The iPad 2 Project Book

Stuff you can do with your iPad

MICHAEL E. COHEN
DENNIS R. COHEN
LISA L. SPANGENBERG

 PEACHPIT PRESS

The iPad 2 Project Book
Michael E. Cohen, Dennis R. Cohen, and Lisa L. Spangenberg

Peachpit Press
1249 Eighth Street
Berkeley, CA 94710
510/524-2178
510/524-2221 (fax)

Find us on the Web at: www.peachpit.com
To report errors, please send a note to errata@peachpit.com.

Peachpit Press is a division of Pearson Education.

Executive editor: Clifford Colby
Editor: Kathy Simpson
Production editor: Danielle Foster
Compositor: Danielle Foster
Indexer: Rebecca Plunkett
Cover design: Peachpit Press
Interior design: Peachpit Press

ISBN-13 978-0-321-77570-2
ISBN-10 0-321-77570-8

9 8 7 6 5 4 3

Printed and bound in the United States of America

Michael and Lisa: *For the late Vinton Dearing, who would be astonished to see what computers can do with text today.*

Dennis: *To my wonderful wife, Kathy, who might love her iPad even more than I love mine (hard to believe, but possible). Also to our kids, grandkids, great-grandkids, and four-legged family members (especially Spenser and Maggie).*

About the Authors

Michael E. Cohen has been (in no particular order) a teacher, a programmer, an editor, a short-order cook, a postal clerk, a Web designer, a digital media producer, an instructional-technology consultant, a certified usability analyst, and an assembly-line worker. A three-time contributing editor of *The Macintosh Bible* and a regular contributor to TidBITS, he co-wrote the *Apple Training Series: iLife '09* and is the author or co-author of several other books. He lives in Santa Monica, California, with about a half-dozen working Macs and the memory board from his Apple Lisa.

Dennis R. Cohen has been developing software since his days with the Jet Propulsion Lab's Deep Space Network and has been writing and editing books and magazine articles since the late 1970s. He's author, co-author, or contributing author of almost 30 titles and the editor of more than 300 technology titles.

Lisa L. Spangenberg, an expert in medieval English and Celtic languages, writes about technology, food, and books when she isn't administering Web servers and creating Web sites. She has wanted an iPad since 2000.

For more information about the authors—and about all things iPad—see their Web site at www.ipadprojectsbook.com.

Acknowledgments

Michael would like to express his thanks to Cliff Colby, who got this book going in a remarkably short time; to Kathy Simpson, who edited his discursive ramblings into something resembling coherent prose; and to the Engsts, who gave him the freedom to work on this project while he had so many other things on his plate.

Dennis would like to thank Apple for creating hardware (like the iPad) that is such a joy to use. Also, thanks to the purveyors of the third-party software that so wonderfully enhances Apple's products—in particular, the iPad. Thanks, too, to Michael and Lisa for providing excellent collaboration on a really enjoyable title. Special thanks to Steven Mowry at the Spokane Apple Store who finally placed an iPad 2 in my anxious hands after my sixth morning waiting in line for a unit.

Lisa would like to thank Mac for food and fresh air, Michael for spiffy introductions and practical advice, and Kathy for making me look much better than I deserve.

Contents

CHAPTER 2 Working and Playing in the iPad

CHAPTER 3　Music, Books, and Movies on the iPad

Introduction

We saw our first iPad in a theater in Hollywood, California, in the summer of 1968. It appeared in the movie *2001: A Space Odyssey*, and the iPad (called a Newspad in the Arthur C. Clarke novel on which the movie is based) made its debut when astronaut Dave Bowman used it to view the news while having a horrific-looking meal of puréed space food. We didn't want any of that food, but boy, did that Newspad look appetizing.

It took only 42 years (interesting number, 42) for the iPad to make it from Hollywood to the Apple Store.

Even more entertaining than the movie were the consternation and confusion among technology pundits when the iPad was announced in 2010. Very few of them could figure out what the device was *for,* and all too many of them were convinced that it wouldn't be popular.

Now we're a year into the iPad era. The iPad has turned out to be even more popular than even the most optimistic pundits expected, and the public has had no problem figuring out what the device is for. In fact, iPad owners have come up with ways to use it that no one expected. (While we were writing this book, for example, a new album recorded and mixed entirely on the iPad went on sale in the iTunes Store.)

What the iPad Is For

What *is* the iPad for? It's for fun. It's for work. It's for convenience. It's for doing whatever a legion of app developers can make a sleek, bright, big-screen, handheld, touch-driven device do: reading books, playing games, looking at photos, looking up at the stars, doing budgets, sending and receiving email, browsing the Web, reserving plane tickets, watching movies or TV, editing video, listening to music, writing music, writing novels or sonnets, drawing pictures, and countless other things.

What This Book Is For

A better question is: What is this *book* you're reading for? It's for showing you how to take advantage of your sleek, bright, big-screen, handheld, touch-driven device.

We call it *The iPad 2 Project Book* because we present this information in the form of projects: simple collections of tasks that you can complete in a few minutes each and that reveal much of your iPad's hidden splendor.

Some projects walk you through basic procedures, like getting your music synced between your computer and your iPad. Other projects help you do fun and useful things with your iPad, like planning a vacation and getting flight reservations.

We've divided the book into the following three chapters:

- **Living in the iPad.** This chapter contains projects that help you perform basic tasks on the iPad, such as syncing your contacts and calendars, setting up security, and handling your mail.

- **Working and Playing in the iPad.** This chapter shows you how to do stuff, such as plan a vacation, and how to make stuff, such as a deck of flash cards that helps you learn another language.

- **Music, Books, and Movies on the iPad.** This chapter contains projects for navigating the various e-book applications you can put on an iPad; putting music, movies, and videos on the iPad; making music and videos with your iPad; and creating e-books to read on your iPad.

This book only scratches the surface of what you can do with your iPad. After all, it's a magical device, and there's a lot you can do with magic.

What's New in This Edition

In this edition, we've eliminated a couple of projects and added a few more, but mostly, we've worked hard to bring all the projects up to date with the current version (4.3.1) of iOS—the operating system that drives the iPad. We've also designed this edition to cover the new, thin, and even more magical iPad 2. If you own the original iPad, though, don't worry. With very few exceptions, everything in this book applies to your iPad too.

A Note About Conventions

Unlike most computer books, this one is short on technical terminology and conventions. Still, there are a few things you need to know.

To begin, even though the iPad works with both Windows PCs and with Macs, all the authors are Mac users. Therefore, the screen shots we provide from computers are from Macs. PCs and Macs are looking more alike all the time, however, so we don't think these screen shots will be a problem for our Windows-using readers.

Also, we tend to use Mac terminology, referring to *dialogs* instead of *dialog boxes*, and we've introduced some iPad-specific terminology, such as *popovers* instead of *drop-down lists*. We're sure that you can figure things out. We also note when Windows and Mac instructions differ (fortunately, fairly seldom) or when instructions for the original iPad differ from those for the iPad 2 (even more fortunately, very rarely).

Sometimes, we say things like "Tap Settings > General > Network." This is a shortcut way of saying, "Tap the Settings app. When Settings opens, tap General; then, in the General screen, tap Network." Again, we're sure that you can figure this out.

Finally, you need to know a few basic iPad action terms:

- **Tap.** Touch your finger to the screen and then quickly lift it.

- **Tap and hold.** Touch the screen and *don't* lift your finger.

- **Swipe.** Touch the screen and quickly drag your finger up, down, left, or right. (We tell you the direction in which to drag.)

And now, with that out of the way, on to the projects.

1

Living in the iPad

Remember how Mary Poppins kept pulling stuff out of her magic little satchel when she first moved into the Banks household? Your iPad is a lot like that satchel.

No, you can't really *live* in your iPad, but it can contain much of the stuff that you use in your daily life and that you ordinarily might keep elsewhere: calendars, address book, mail, notebooks, and so on. This stuff would be really useful to have on an iPad.

That's what this chapter is about: projects that show you how to get your stuff into and out of your iPad, as well as a few cool things you can do with that stuff after it takes up residence on the iPad.

Information Syncing Project

Difficulty level: Easy

Software needed: iTunes

iPad model: Any

Additional hardware: None

If you've been using a computer for any length of time, it probably stores a lot of information that you use regularly, such as contact lists, browser bookmarks, calendars, and notes. This information would be *really* useful to have on your iPad—not just have on your iPad, but also have there in such a way that you can get any changes you make on the iPad back on your computer.

Doing this information shuffle with your iPad is easy, but first, you have to make it possible. Setting things up so that your computer and iPad can exchange your information is what this simple project is for.

The act of getting your information from your computer to your iPad and back is called *syncing* (short for *synchronizing*), and it's more than just a simple matter of copying your stuff from your computer to your iPad or from your iPad to your computer.

Syncing involves looking at two similar sets of information (such as the contacts in your address book on your computer and the contacts on your iPad), figuring out what's different between those two sets, and sorting things so that the differences between those two sets of infor- mation are resolved. Contacts that you created on your iPad go to your computer, for example; contacts that you created on your computer go to your iPad; and contacts that you changed on one device or the other are brought into alignment.

In Apple's world of handheld devices, the key to getting your stuff from here to there and back again is iTunes.

Yes, we know—things like contact lists, appointment books, and browser bookmarks aren't songs, so it does seem a little odd (OK, *more* than a little odd) to use iTunes to move them back and forth between your computer and your iPad. Don't question. That's just the way it is. Embrace it.

So how do you sync your iPad and your computer? Simple: Connect them with the dock connector, and stand back. Unless you've fiddled around with the default settings, iTunes opens and automatically syncs the two devices. It does this each and every time you connect your iPad to your computer.

tip **Any time you don't want iTunes to sync your iPad and your computer automatically, you can hold down the Option and Command keys (Mac) or the Shift and Ctrl keys (Windows) when you connect your iPad. Keep holding those keys down until your iPad appears in the iTunes Source list.**

View your sync settings

Your iPad can sync with a lot of sources in a lot of ways—directly over the air with MobileMe, for example, or with Google. You can mix and match syncing methods, but the number of combinations can become complex. In this project, we're going to go with the simplest case: syncing by way of direct connection between your iPad and your computer.

First, you connect your iPad to your computer and confirm a general option that controls how your iPad and iTunes interact.

Connecting your iPad and viewing general options:

1. Connect your iPad to your computer with the dock connector.

   If you haven't changed any of the default settings for the iPad or iTunes, iTunes begins syncing with your iPad after a few seconds, and the iPad appears in the iTunes Source list—that's the sidebar on the left side of the iTunes window—below the Devices heading (**Figure 1.1** on the next page). Go ahead and let it sync; that won't hurt anything.

 In addition to syncing, iTunes backs up the information on your iPad every time you connect it. This backup takes place before any information is synced.

Figure 1.1 The iPad appears in the iTunes Source list when you connect it to your computer.

Source list

2. Select your iPad in the iTunes Source list.

In the main iTunes display on the right, a Summary pane appears (**Figure 1.2**). This pane gives you information about your iPad and offers you a variety of options.

Figure 1.2 The iTunes Summary pane for an iPad is more than just a summary; it also has options you can set.

3. Make sure that the check box titled Open iTunes when this iPad is connected is checked.

    This setting is the best one to use if you want to sync your iPad with iTunes regularly.

The other options aren't relevant for syncing your general information with your iPad. You can ignore them for now (but not forever).

The real fun stuff is on the pane associated with the Info button, which is located in the header area at the top of the main iTunes display. That pane is where you set up syncing for your contacts, calendars, book-marks, mail settings, and notes.

Sync contacts

First, you need to set up contact syncing. iTunes knows about various contact sources on your computer and on the Internet, and it allows you to pick which ones to sync with your iPad, depending on your oper-ating system:

-   **On a Mac,** you can sync from Address Book as well as from other contact sources, such as Yahoo Address Book and Google Contacts.

-   **In Windows,** you can sync from only one source of contacts at a time. Your options include Yahoo Address Book, Google Contacts, Windows Address Book (Microsoft Outlook Express), Windows Vista Contacts, and Microsoft Outlook (2003, 2007, or 2010).

 On both a Mac and a Windows PC, you can organize your contacts in groups. iPad contact syncing lets you sync only specific groups of contacts, if you like.

Setting contact sync options:

1. Make sure that the iPad is connected to your computer, that iTunes is open, and that the iPad is selected in the iTunes Source list.

    This will be the case if you just completed the steps in "Connecting your iPad and viewing general options" earlier in this project.

2. Above the main iTunes display, click the Info button.

    Near the top of the Info pane, a panel displays the contact syncing options. The options in this panel differ, depending on whether you have a Mac or a PC running Windows.

3. Do one of the following:

    • **On a Mac,** check Sync Address Book Contacts (**Figure 1.3**).

Figure 1.3 The contact syncing options on the Mac allow you to sync from several contact sources at the same time.

    • **In Windows,** check Sync contacts from and then choose the source of the contacts that you want to sync from the menu. Depending on the source you choose, you may have to enter login credentials so that iTunes and your iPad can access the contacts.

4. If you want to sync only specific contact groups, click Selected groups and then check the contact groups that you want to appear on your iPad; otherwise, click All contacts.

5. If you want the new contacts you create on your iPad to belong to a specific contact group, check the box titled Add contacts created outside of groups on this iPad to; then choose a group from the pop-up menu.

6. (Optional) On a Mac, check Sync Yahoo! Address Book contacts and then enter your Yahoo login information.

7. (Optional) Also on a Mac, check Sync Google Contacts and then enter your Google login information.

    When you apply these changes, described later in this project, iTunes syncs your iPad with the new settings.

Sync calendars

When your contact sync settings are squared away, the next step is setting up the calendars that you want to sync. Depending on your operating system, do this:

- **On a Mac,** you can sync your iCal calendars, which can include calendars from any application that syncs with iCal.

- **In Windows,** you can choose to sync calendars with Microsoft Outlook 2003, 2007, or 2010.

Setting calendar sync options:

1. On the Info pane, do one of the following:

   - **On a Mac,** check Sync iCal Calendars (**Figure 1.4**).

Figure 1.4 The calendar syncing options allow you to choose specific calendars.

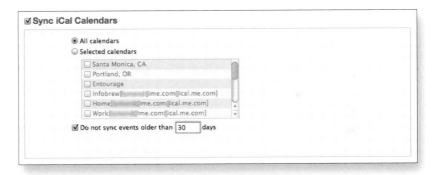

   - **In Windows,** check Sync calendars with; then, from the drop-down menu, choose the application that manages the calendars you want to sync.

2. If you want to sync only specific calendars, click Selected calendars and then check the calendars that you want to appear on your iPad; otherwise, click All calendars.

3. (Optional) Click Do not sync events older than *x* days and then enter a number in the text box.

 tip   **Unless you think you'll need to refer to past events on your iPad, choosing not to sync events older than 30 days (the default) helps keep your iPad calendar uncluttered.**

Sync mail settings

First, let's be clear: iTunes does *not* sync mail between your iPad and your computer. Instead, both your computer and your iPad obtain and display your email directly from your email provider (or providers; Michael currently has email accounts with four providers, for example).

What iTunes *does* sync are the settings you've enabled for each of your email accounts. This feature is a shortcut, really: It helps you skip the sometimes-confusing task of specifying settings for each email account manually on your iPad by copying those settings directly from your computer.

 Apple calls this process syncing, but the syncing goes only one way: from your computer to your iPad. If you change email settings on your iPad, they don't sync back to your computer.

Although a plethora of email programs is available for both Mac and Windows, iTunes can sync settings from only a few of those programs—specifically, Mail on a Mac and Microsoft Outlook (2003, 2007, or 2010) or Outlook Express on a PC.

If you have and use any of the iTunes-blessed mail programs, you can quickly get your mail settings onto your iPad.

Syncing mail settings:

1.   On the Info pane, check Sync Mail Accounts (**Figure 1.5**).

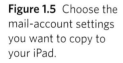 **Figure 1.5** Choose the mail-account settings you want to copy to your iPad.

2.   In the list of mail accounts, check each account that contains settings you want to sync to your iPad.

Sync notes and bookmarks

The iPad has a built-in browser (Mobile Safari) and a note-taking app (Notes), and you can sync bookmarks and notes from these apps between your iPad and your computer, based on your operating system:

- **On a Mac,** you can sync your bookmarks between Mobile Safari on the iPad and Safari. (Sorry, Mozilla Firefox fans—no soup for you.)

- **In Windows,** you can sync bookmarks between your iPad and either Safari or Internet Explorer. (*Still* no soup for you, Firefox fans.)

The notes you create on your iPad can sync to the Mail application on the Mac or to Microsoft Outlook in Windows, and vice versa.

Syncing notes and bookmarks:

1. In the Other section of the Info pane, check the bookmark syncing option you prefer:

   - **On a Mac,** your only choice is Safari.

   - **In Windows,** you can choose Internet Explorer or (if it's installed) Safari.

2. Check the notes-syncing option.

From now on, whenever you make or change a note on your iPad, or add a bookmark, the info gets synced to your computer. Similarly, any notes or bookmarks that you add or change on your computer (if you're using one of the iTunes-supported programs) appear on your iPad the next time you sync.

Apply your sync settings

Finally, it's time to apply the settings that you specified and get your iPad resynced the way you want it.

Applying sync-settings changes:

1. In the bottom-right corner of the Info pane, click Apply.

   iTunes applies the changes you made and syncs your iPad.

2. When the sync is complete, disconnect your iPad.

   The iPad disappears from the iTunes Source list, and you're ready to go enjoy your newly synced iPad.

In the future, whenever you connect your iPad to your computer, the sync settings you made in this project are in effect, syncing just the information you want to sync between your iPad and your computer.

 If you never want your iPad to sync with your computer when you connect it, open iTunes Preferences (choose iTunes > Preferences on a Mac or Edit > Preferences in Windows), click Devices, and select Prevent iPods, iPhones, and iPads from syncing automatically.

Why iTunes for Syncing?

If you *really* want to know why you use iTunes to sync so much nonmusic stuff, the answer has to do with history and evolution.

In the beginning, there was iTunes, which stored and played your music for you.

Next came the iPod, a music-playing device, and it seemed only natural for Apple to use iTunes as the software that moved music from your computer to that device. Also, because the iPod had a screen that could display text, Apple provided—just as an extra-special bonus—the ability to copy contacts and calendars from your computer to your iPod so that you could have them with you as you walked around listening to your music.

But the iPod soon developed more capabilities, such as the ability to show video, so Apple added video playback to iTunes and enabled iTunes to share that video with the iPod.

Then came the iPhone, which was like an iPod from the future: It could not only play music and video and display text, but also handle email, create appointments and contacts, browse the Web, and run applications. So Apple gave iTunes the ability to sync contacts and calendars and apps and bookmarks between the iPhone and the computer.

After that came the iPad, which can handle even more kinds of information, and Apple grafted the ability to sync those kinds of information onto iTunes as well.

That's where we are today, with the distant descendant of the original music-playing application managing all sorts of information on the distant descendant of the original handheld music-playing device: evolution and intelligent design joining hands, wearing white earbuds, and dancing together. We get all misty just thinking about it.

Wireless Syncing Project

Difficulty level: Intermediate

Software needed: MobileMe account

iPad model: Any

Additional hardware: None

When you begin living with your iPad, you soon discover that it's really convenient to put a lot of the personal information that you keep on your desktop or laptop computer on your iPad as well. The preceding **Information Syncing Project** shows how to bring all that stuff into alignment every time you connect your iPad to your computer.

But using that method of syncing your information means that you *have* to connect your iPad to your computer every so often to keep each device up to date, and for best results, you need do this regularly and frequently. It's just like brushing your teeth.

We live, however, in an age of miracles and wonder—and of wireless technology. There's no reason why your iPad and your computer can't share their information over the air so you can avoid the daily chore of getting them all synced up. (You should still brush your teeth, of course.)

No matter whether you have a Wi-Fi or 3G iPad, you can make use of cloud services to sync your information between your computer and your iPad. (To find out what we mean by *cloud services,* see the nearby sidebar "What Is This Cloud of Which You Speak?") This project describes how to use a cloud service offered by Apple: MobileMe. In this project, you sync your contacts, calendars, and bookmarks with MobileMe from both your computer and your iPad.

 If you already have a MobileMe account and use it to sync your contacts, calendars, and bookmarks between your computer and MobileMe, you can skip the next two sections and go right to "Cut the cord." Otherwise, read on.

Get a MobileMe account

To use a cloud-based service, you need to have an account with that service, such as Apple's MobileMe.

A MobileMe account is free for the first 60 days so that you can try out the service; it costs $99 a year after that. If you have a Mac, Apple makes it very easy to get a MobileMe account; if you don't already have one, you've probably been asked by your Mac to set one up on more than one occasion.

Sync Outside the Box

MobileMe isn't your only wireless syncing option for your iPad, of course. You can use one of these services instead:

- **Google.** Google supports wireless syncing with its services. You can find out more at the Google Sync page (www.google.com/support/mobile/bin/topic.py?hl=en&topic=14252).

- **Microsoft Exchange.** Readers who use a Microsoft Exchange server for school or business aren't left out of the party either, because the iPad can sync with an Exchange account. Although the setup process usually is simple, you should consult the Exchange server's administrator to see whether it's configured to support iPad users.

Signing up for MobileMe:

- **On a Mac,** open System Preferences, click the MobileMe icon, and follow the onscreen instructions.

- **In Windows,** go to www.apple.com/mobileme, and click the prominently displayed Sign up for MobileMe Free Trial button. When you create a MobileMe account in Windows, Apple provides a MobileMe control panel for your Windows system so that you can control the service's various features.

 MobileMe's features—both on the Mac and in Windows—include email; contacts; calendars; gigabytes of file storage on Apple's servers; and quite a bit more, including a valuable Find My iPhone/iPad service that you can use to locate your device, should you lose it.

Go from computer to cloud

Now that you have a MobileMe account, you need to sync your information between it and your computer so that your iPad can get your information from MobileMe, as follows:

- **On a Mac,** you can sync your contacts from Address Book, your calendars from iCal, and your bookmarks from Safari.

- **In Windows,** you can sync your contacts from Microsoft Outlook 2003, 2007, or 2010 (32-bit); from Vista Contacts; or from Windows Address Book. You sync your calendars from Outlook; if you use another calendar program, you need to move your calendar events to Outlook if you want to sync them with MobileMe. You can sync your bookmarks from either Internet Explorer or Safari. (Yes, Apple offers a Windows version of Safari.)

 If you currently have a MobileMe account and already sync your Mac or PC data with MobileMe, skip to "Cut the cord," a few pages ahead.

 After you sync your information between your computer and MobileMe, you can access it from any computer with a modern Web browser. Just go to www.me.com and log in.

What Is This Cloud of Which You Speak?

Cloud is one of those terms that has moved out of the cloistered halls of geekdom into the light of day. It really means nothing more than *somewhere on the Internet, outside your local network.* The term comes from the cloud-shaped symbol used in the network diagrams that networking professionals draw from time to time when they get tired of reading router logs. Like a real-world cloud, a virtual cloud is a shapeless object—one into which you can't easily see.

In this project, *cloud* refers to the Apple servers on which your iPad information is stored so that you can get to it from anywhere on the Internet.

Syncing from a Mac with MobileMe:

1. Open System Preferences, and click MobileMe.

2. In the MobileMe window, click the Sync tab.

3. Select the Synchronize with MobileMe check box, and choose Automatically from the adjacent pop-up menu.

   When you choose Automatically, your Mac and MobileMe will sync information as soon as you change it.

4. In the list of items that you can sync, select Bookmarks, Calendars, and Contacts (**Figure 1.6**).

Figure 1.6 The Sync tab of the MobileMe System Preferences window in Mac OS X.

5. Click the Sync Now button.

6. Close System Preferences.

   Your Mac sends your information to the cloud, ready to be synced with your iPad (or with any other computers and devices that you sync with the same MobileMe account).

 If you use iCal and have never synced with MobileMe, read the nearby sidebar "Using iCal with the New MobileMe Calendar" to see how to get your On My Mac iCal events into MobileMe.

Using iCal with the New MobileMe Calendar

In the olden days, when you bought a MobileMe subscription and told iCal to sync with MobileMe, the events in your calendars located in iCal's On My Mac collection would sync with MobileMe. In 2010, however, Apple changed how MobileMe calendars worked and provided an upgrade process to move those synced On My Mac calendars to a new MobileMe collection in iCal. You've probably already received email from Apple explaining how to upgrade your iCal calendars.

That upgrade process, however, works only for those who have previously synced their On My Mac calendars with MobileMe. If you use iCal and have never synced your On My Mac calendars with MobileMe, you have to export each On My Mac calendar and then import it into a new MobileMe calendar if you want to sync it with MobileMe. Here's how you do that:

1. In iCal, select a calendar in the On My Mac collection of calendars and then choose File > Export > Export.

2. In the window that appears, give the exported calendar a name, and choose where to save it (temporarily) on your Mac.

3. In iCal, choose File > New Calendar and then choose your MobileMe account from the New Calendar submenu.

   A new, untitled calendar appears in the MobileMe collection in iCal's sidebar.

4. Rename the untitled calendar.

   You can use the name you used for the On My Mac calendar that you exported.

5. Choose File > Import > Import, select the calendar that you exported, and then click Import.

6. In the Add Events window that appears, choose the new MobileMe calendar from the pop-up menu, and click OK.

When you complete that last step, iCal imports the calendar into your new MobileMe calendar. In the future, any events you add to this calendar automatically sync with MobileMe. If you like, you can delete the calendar that you exported from your Mac and deselect the old On My Mac version of the calendar in iCal's sidebar.

Syncing from a Windows PC with MobileMe:

1. Choose Start > Control Panel to open Control Panel.

2. In the Network and Internet section, choose the MobileMe control panel.

3. Sign in with the MobileMe member name and password that you created when you set up your MobileMe account.

4. Click the Sync tab.

5. Select Sync with MobileMe, and choose Automatically from the drop-down menu.

6. Select Contacts, and choose the application that manages your contacts from the drop-down menu.

7. Select Calendars, and choose the calendar application from the drop-down menu.

8. Select Bookmarks, and choose the Web browser that you use from the drop-down menu.

9. Click the Sync Now button.

10. Close the MobileMe control panel.

Cut the cord

Reading this section is necessary only if you've completed the **Information Syncing Project** earlier in this chapter. In this section, you undo what you did in the earlier project: You turn off wired syncing of contacts, calendars, and bookmarks between your iPad and your computer.

 Most likely, nothing will go wrong if you don't turn off wired syncing of your information. When you sync the same information over a dock-connector cable with iTunes and wirelessly with MobileMe, however, you may end up with duplicate information.

Turning off wired syncing of your information:

1. Launch iTunes, if it's not already running.

2. Connect your iPad, and let the sync take place.

   After the sync, your iPad and your computer have the same information. What's more, your computer and MobileMe should also be in sync if you set up MobileMe to sync automatically (as we show you how to do in "Go from computer to cloud" earlier in this project).

3. In the iTunes Source list, select your iPad.

4. At the top of the main iTunes pane, click the Info button.

5. Clear the check box titled Sync Address Book Contacts (Mac) or Sync Contacts (Windows).

6. Clear the check box titled Sync iCal Calendars (Mac) or Sync Calendars (Windows).

7. In the Other section, clear the check box titled Sync Safari Bookmarks (Mac) or the corresponding check box in Windows.

    In Windows, the name of this option depends on the browser with which you sync bookmarks. Internet Explorer, for example, calls bookmarks *favorites*, so if you use it to sync bookmarks, this option would be called Sync Favorites.

8. Disconnect your iPad from the dock-connector cable.

Go from cloud to iPad

Now you're ready to set up your MobileMe account on your iPad and activate contact, calendar, and bookmark syncing. If you previously synced these items with iTunes, you also specify what to do with the information that remains on your iPad.

Creating a MobileMe account on the iPad:

1. On the iPad, tap the Settings app.

2. In the pane on the left side of the Settings screen, tap Mail, Contacts, Calendars.

3. In the Accounts section of the resulting screen, tap Add Account.

4. In the Add Account screen, tap MobileMe.

    An account-entry form appears (**Figure 1.7** on the next page).

5. Tap and type to enter the requested information: the email address assigned to your MobileMe account and the password for your MobileMe account.

6. Tap the Next button in the top-right corner.

    A second account form appears, in which you can turn MobileMe features on or off for your account.

7. Tap the Contacts switch in the form to turn on contacts syncing.

    If you have any contacts on your iPad (and you probably do, if you've completed the **Information Syncing Project** earlier in this chapter), a Merge Contacts dialog appears, asking you what to do with any existing contacts on your iPad (**Figure 1.8**).

Figure 1.8 The Merge Contacts dialog asks you to merge your iPad information with MobileMe.

8. If you see the Merge Contacts dialog, tap the Merge button.

    If you've worked through the preceding sections of this project, the contacts on your iPad already are the same as the ones in MobileMe, so merging should have no effect; identical contacts are ignored.

9. Tap the Calendars switch, and if the Merge Calendars dialog appears, tap the Merge button.

    Again, if you followed the instructions earlier in this project, the calendars on your iPad should already match those in MobileMe, so merging them has no effect.

10. Tap the Bookmarks switch to open the Merge Bookmarks dialog.

11. Tap the Merge button.

12. Tap the Save button in the top-right corner of the MobileMe account form.

    The form closes, and you return to the Mail, Contacts, Calendars page.

13. Tap Fetch New Data.

14. In the screen that appears, tap the Push switch to turn it on.

    When Push is turned on, MobileMe gets in touch with your iPad whenever mail is sent to your MobileMe address, no matter whether your iPad is awake or asleep—as long as your iPad is connected to the Internet, that is.

15. Press the Home button on your iPad.

    Now your iPad and MobileMe are set to communicate. Whenever you make a change in your calendars, contacts, or bookmarks on your computer, the change is sent to your iPad over the Internet. Similarly, any changes you make in your contacts, calendars, or bookmarks on your iPad are sent over the Internet to your computer. It's magical!

Mail Management Project

Difficulty level: Easy

Software needed: Working email account (free or paid), MobileMe account (optional; $99 per year)

iPad model: Any

Additional hardware: None

The iPad, aside from its many other virtues, is a useful device for reading, responding to, and managing your email at those times when you aren't shackled to your computer (and how sweet those times can be!).

Managing your email on your iPad is much easier, however, if you use the IMAP email protocol. Most Web-mail applications use IMAP (see the sidebar "IMAP and POP Mail Accounts" later in this project for details), which means that your email is synchronized across devices automatically. If you sync your email accounts and contacts via iTunes or MobileMe, you may not even have to add any accounts to your iPad by hand, but you may want to stop right now and check out the **Information Syncing Project** earlier in this chapter to make sure that your account data is the same on your iPad as it is on your other devices.

 In the following pages, we use the word *folder* **to refer to what is sometimes called a mailbox or directory, simply because the iPad icon for mailboxes and mail directories is a folder, one of which is named Inbox. The terms are really equivalents in practical terms.**

Add contacts

The easiest way to add contacts to the Contacts app on your iPad initially is to sync with your contacts on your computer, via iTunes or MobileMe. But Mail has a couple of smart ways to make adding contacts much easier than filling out the Contact screen by hand (though that's always an option too).

The second-easiest way is to add contacts from emails you receive. You can add information to any extant contact or create a new contact based on information in an email, as we show you in the following tasks.

Adding contacts from email address fields:

1. Find an email in your Inbox (or any other mail folder on your iPad) containing an address that you want to add to your Contacts app.

    You're going to create a new contact entry for that address.

2. Tap the person's name or email address in the From, To, or CC field of the email.

    You see a popover similar to the one shown in **Figure 1.9**. If you tapped the From field, this window is titled Sender; if you tapped the To field, it's Recipient; and if you tapped the CC field, it's CC. Your contact form may have more or less information than the one shown in the figure.

Figure 1.9 Using the From line in an email to create a new contact.

The email address used in the email is already filled in for you. Below the address are two buttons: Create New Contact and Add to Existing Contact.

3. Tap Create New Contact.

The popover (Sender, Recipient, or CC) is replaced by the New Contact form (**Figure 1.10**).

Figure 1.10
New Contact form.

tip The Contacts app works in part by matching email addresses, so if you have a contact who has more than one email address, you may accidentally create a second contact for that person. When in doubt, tap the Add to Existing Contact button instead of Create New Contact. You'll see a list of all your contacts in a popover. If the contact doesn't already exist, just tap Cancel, and you'll return to the popover shown in Figure 1.9, where you can tap Create New Contact.

4. Fill out the First and Last name fields (if your correspondent doesn't use them as part of his or her email address).

5. Tap the blue Done button in the top-right corner to save the new contact information and close the New Contact form.

You'll see a contact form similar to **Figure 1.11.** You can edit the information in this form, as we show you in the following task.

Figure 1.11
Contact form.

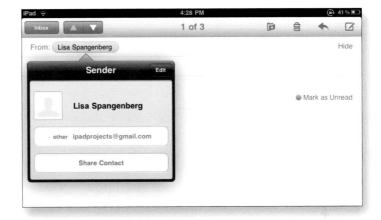

Editing a contact created from an email address:

1. Tap the Edit button in the contact form (refer to Figure 1.11) to edit or add to the existing information.

    The form expands as shown in **Figure 1.12**.

Figure 1.12 Expanding a contact form.

2. Edit or enter new information in any of the fields.

3. If you want to add an image to the contact, tap the Add Photo rectangle in the top-left corner, and insert an image from the iPad's Photos app.

For more projects that use the Photos app, see Chapter 3.

4. Tap the blue Done button in the top-right corner to save your changes and close the form.

Adding contact data from an email body:

1. Find an email with an email address in its body that you want to add to a contact.

You can also add a street address, phone number, or URL (see the nearby sidebar "Adding Other Kinds of Data to Contacts from Mail"), but in this task, we're going to show you how to add an email address. The basic procedure for adding all the other types of contact data is the same, though the contact form will look slightly different for each type.

2. Tap and hold the address until you see a popover similar to the one shown in **Figure 1.13**.

Figure 1.13 Contact options for an address in an email body.

Adding Other Kinds of Data to Contacts from Mail

Quite often, the body of an email someone sends you contains information that you want to incorporate into a contact, such as a name and address, a phone number, or a URL. In most cases, Mail recognizes that the http:// and www. prefixes identify a Web site, that phone numbers and street addresses have particular combinations of characters and formatting, and that email addresses use the @ sign. Consequently, when you tap a phone number, a URL, or an email address, Mail tries to predict what you're likely to want to do with it—such as add it to a contact or create a new contact.

Here are a few things you can do with contact data in email:

- If you tap and hold a URL, you see options to open that URL in Safari or copy it to almost anything on your iPad that accepts text, such as a contact or a new email message. If you simply tap a URL, Safari launches and attempts to go to the Web page associated with the URL you tapped.

- If you tap and hold a street address, the options are Open in Maps, which displays a Google street map; Create a New Contact; Add to Contact, which directs Mail to put the address information in the correct fields of the contact form (a task that Mail sometimes has difficulties with); and Copy, which allows you to use the copied address elsewhere. If you simply tap the address, Safari launches and attempts to locate the address in the Maps app.

- If you tap a phone number (domestic or international), you see the options Create New Contact and Add to Existing Contact.

The "tap and hold" part is important. If you merely tap an email address, Mail assumes that you want to send an email immediately, so it creates a blank email form with the tapped address placed in the To field.

3. Tap one of the following buttons to accomplish the associated task:

   - **New Message,** which creates a new email for you, already addressed to the email address you tapped

   - **Create New Contact,** which opens a New Contact form with the email address already filled in (refer to Figure 1.9 earlier in this project)

- **Add to Existing Contact,** which lets you select and modify an existing contact in the Contacts app

- **Copy,** which places the email address on the iPad's clipboard so that you can paste it into another application or a draft email

At the bottom of every contact form, just to the right of the Edit button, is a Share button. Tap this button to attach a .vcf (vCard) file to an email. The recipient can automatically add the information in the vCard to his Contacts app or another contact database that supports the .vcf format. We show you how to use this feature in the next task.

Sharing a contact entry:

1. Open an entry in the Contacts app that you want to share via email (**Figure 1.14**).

Figure 1.14 Contact form with Share button visible.

2. Tap the Share button in the bottom-right corner.

   (You may have to scroll down the form to see the Share button, depending on how much information the contact contains.)

Lisa Spangenberg.vcf

You see a blank email form, ready to be addressed, that includes a vCard attachment. The icon for the vCard looks like a small card with a blue human figure.

3. Complete the email form by adding a recipient and a message; then send it.

   Your recipient probably can simply tap (on an iPad) or double-click the icon to add that information to her own contacts list.

> **note** **Information in the contact's Notes field on the iPad isn't included in the shared vCard.**

Draft an email

Sometimes when you're writing an email, you need to set it aside and return to it later. Mail will save a copy of an unfinished email for you as a draft. You can find it in the special Drafts folder in the account that would have sent the mail, had you finished writing and tapped Send.

Saving a draft email:

1. Tap the gray Cancel button in the top-left corner of the email form.

   You see a popover with a red Delete Draft button and a gray Save Draft button (**Figure 1.15**).

Figure 1.15 Email draft options.

Mail Shortcuts for Addresses and Photos

We're assuming that you've already set up Mail on your iPad to send and receive email. You've got the basics down; you know how to reply to an email you've received, initiate a new email by tapping the Compose icon, and send your finished email by tapping Send. But the iPad can make emailing easier for you in a couple of ways:

- When you start typing an address in the To field of an email, for example, the iPad, working with the Contacts app, tries to guess the person you're going to send the email to. The results can include people you've corresponded with, even though they aren't listed in your Contacts app.

- If you know exactly whom you want to email, it may be more efficient to tap the blue plus-sign icon at the right end of the To field, scroll through your Contacts app, and select that person's email address.

- If you want to email an image to someone, you can use the Photos app, like so:

  1. Tap the Photos app's icon to launch the app on your iPad.

  2. Find the image you want to send, and tap the curved-arrow Action button in the top-right corner.

     You see a popover with several buttons, including Email Photo.

  3. Tap Email Photo.

     The iPad switches to Mail, where the image is already attached to a blank email form.

  4. Add an address, subject, and message body.

  5. Send the finished email.

     You're back at the image you selected in step 2.

  2. Tap Save Draft.

     The draft is saved to the Drafts folder for that email account.

Manage your mailboxes

If you have multiple devices that can check email and multiple email accounts, the best mail-management tip we can offer you is to let your email server manage mail for you. Leaving your mail on the server and letting the server be the primary email source means that you'll see the same mailboxes—and find the same messages in the same read or unread states—on all your devices.

Navigating your mailboxes may mean navigating multiple email accounts. The iPad Mail app has a separate Inbox for each account, as well as a unified All Inboxes folder that displays the Inbox contents for all email accounts. (For more information on the latter folder, see the "All Inboxes" sidebar at the end of this project.)

Another challenge associated with email is spam. People we don't know send us email we don't want. When you scan your Inbox, one way to isolate the real mail from spam (some legitimate bulk mail sent to mailing lists isn't spam) is to see whether a particular piece of mail was sent to you alone or to you and a bunch of other people. In the following task, we show you how.

IMAP and POP Mail Accounts

When you send mail, your email client and Internet service provider (ISP) use a protocol called SMTP (Simple Mail Transfer Protocol). But when you set up your iPad to receive mail, you usually have the option of telling Mail to use IMAP (Internet Message Access Protocol) or POP (Post Office Protocol) for each email account you set up. In some cases, though, you don't have a choice; your IT department at work or your ISP will tell you which protocol to use for incoming mail.

Here are some things to keep in mind about how POP and IMAP work:

- **IMAP** is designed to leave mail on the server and to make sure that every device that logs on to the server has exactly the same mail in the same folders. IMAP accounts let your organize your email in very elaborate ways. You can have lots of folders, and even folders within folders, if you want.

- **POP** is designed to delete email from the server as soon as it has been downloaded to your computer. This arrangement is awkward if you read mail on multiple devices, because you won't see the same incoming emails on all of them. The solution is to make your main computer the one that controls when email is deleted from the server. (A setting in Mail and other email clients tells the server how long to leave incoming mail on the server.) On your other devices that use that POP account, set the time for deleting email to be never—or at least longer than the time you set for your main computer.

You can find a useful explanation of the differences between (and benefits of) POP and IMAP here:

http://docs.info.apple.com/article.html?path=Mail/3.0/en/11920.html

Turning on Show To/Cc Label to check for spam:

1. Launch the Settings app on your iPad to open the Settings screen.

2. Tap Mail, Contacts, Calendars in the Settings column.

   You see the pane shown in **Figure 1.16**.

Figure 1.16 The Mail, Contacts, Calendars pane.

3. Tap the switch to the right of Show To/Cc Label to set it to On (**Figure 1.17**).

Figure 1.17 Set the Show To/Cc Label switch to On.

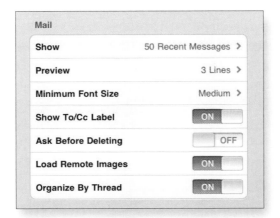

From now on, popovers listing mail in your Inbox and other mail folders display a small gray To icon next to messages addressed only to you.

Deleting a single email:

1. Open an email that you want to delete.

2. Tap the trash-can icon in the top-right corner of the message.

The email shrinks and disappears into the trash can in what Apple calls the *genie effect*.

If you happen to delete an email by mistake and realize your error immediately (or very soon thereafter), you can recover the email by opening the Trash folder associated with the account in question (by tapping the trash-can icon) and moving the email from Trash to your Inbox.

Depending on your email account settings and the settings of your ISP's mail server, mail that you delete on your iPad may remain in a Deleted Email or Trash folder for a while. Deleting the email in that folder should get rid of it permanently.

You can also delete or move several emails from one mail folder to another at the same time, as we show you in the next task.

Deleting multiple emails:

1. Tap a mail folder on your iPad.

    You see a popover similar to the one shown in **Figure 1.18**.

Figure 1.18 A mail list in Mail.

2. Tap the Edit button in the top-right corner of the popover.

    You see a new popover listing the email in that folder, with a circle to the left of each message (**Figure 1.19**).

Figure 1.19 A mail list, ready to be edited.

Circles

3. Tap the circle to the left of a message that you want to delete.

    The circle turns red with a white check in its center (**Figure 1.20**).

Figure 1.20 Selecting
mail for deletion.

4. Repeat step 3 to select as many emails as you want.

5. When you've selected all the emails that you want to delete, tap the
    red Delete button at the bottom of the popover.

    The selected emails disappear (via the genie effect) into the top-left
    corner of the popover.

note For a Gmail account, you may see a red Archive button instead of a Delete button on iPads using iOS 4.2 and later. Archived mail is placed in your Gmail account's All Mail folder. To delete mail, move it to the Gmail account's Trash folder. You can disable this feature by choosing iPad Settings > Mail, Contacts, Calendars > Gmail Account > Archive Messages.

tip Any time you see a list of emails in a floating Mail window, you can swipe a finger across an individual email in the list and then tap the red Delete button to delete it. Tap the blue Done button when you're ready to return to reading email.

Moving a single email to a different folder:

1. Open an email that you want to move from one mailbox to another.

 2. Tap the folder icon in the top-right section of the window.

   You see a popover listing your mail folders, similar to the one shown in **Figure 1.21** (though likely with very different folders).

Figure 1.21 List of mail folders for a single email account.

3. Tap the folder to which you want to move the open email.

   The email shrinks into that folder via the genie effect.

Moving multiple emails to a single folder:

1. Open a mail folder.

   You see a popover listing the mail in that folder (similar to the one shown in Figure 1.18 earlier in this project).

2. Tap the Edit button in the top-right corner of the popover.

   You see a new popover (similar to the one shown in Figure 1.19 earlier in this project).

3. Select the messages you want to move by tapping them.

   The gray circle to the immediate left of each selected email becomes a red circle with a white check in it (**Figure 1.22**).

Figure 1.22 Selecting multiple emails in a list to be moved to a new folder.

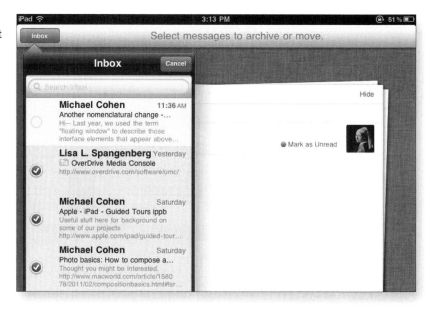

4. Tap the blue Move button in the bottom-right corner of the popover (not visible in Figure 1.22).

   You see a list of mail folders similar to the one shown in Figure 1.21 earlier in this project.

5. Tap the destination mailbox or folder in the popover.

   You see the emails shrink into that folder via the genie effect, and the iPad returns you to your open email.

All Inboxes

Mail now has an universal Inbox called All Inboxes that lists the mail in all the account Inboxes. Here's how you use it:

1. Tap the Mailbox button in the top-left corner of the All Inboxes window to display a popover list of Mail's Inboxes and, below that, a list of all the accounts (**Figure 1.23**).

Figure 1.23 List of mail inboxes and accounts.

2. Tap an Inbox to see just that account's Inbox.

3. Tap an account to see a hierarchical list of all that account's mailboxes.

4. Tap a mailbox to see its contents.

Contact and Calendar Management Project

Difficulty level: Easy

Software needed: None

iPad model: Any

Additional hardware: None

Earlier projects in this chapter show you how to move your information from your computer *to* your iPad. This simple project helps you arrange and view your information in different ways after it's on your iPad.

Suppose that you like to look up your contacts by first name, and we like to look up ours by last name. Although this scenario may seem like a case of "You say *po-tay-toe,* and I say *po-tah-toe,*" wars have been fought over less. (No, really! Check out the War of Jenkins' Ear.) Therefore, in an attempt to foster universal harmony and peace among all people of goodwill, follow along as we show you the simple settings you can control to tailor the way you interact with your information on your iPad.

Sort your contacts

Our trivial example is actually not so trivial. A business user may want her contacts to be arranged by surname, just as in a phone book or a corporate directory, but someone whose contacts list consists mostly of friends and relatives may well want to find his contacts by those names he knows best: first names.

You can sort your contacts either way. What's more, no matter how you sort them, the iPad offers a way to present those contacts with the first name shown either before or after the last name.

Changing the sort order and presentation of contact names:

1.   Tap Settings > Mail, Contacts, Calendars.

2.   In the Mail, Contacts, Calendars screen, swipe down until you see the Contacts section (**Figure 1.24**).

Figure 1.24 The sort settings for contacts are near the bottom of the screen.

3. Tap Sort Order to open the Sort Order screen.

4. Tap the sort order that you prefer.

5. At the top of the Sort Order screen, tap Mail, Contacts, Calendars and then tap Display Order.

6. In the resulting Display Order screen, tap the display order that you prefer.

   In case you don't know what we (and the iPad) mean by *display order,* see **Figure 1.25**.

Figure 1.25 Two of this book's authors listed in the Contacts app in each of the available display orders.

| Dennis **Cohen** | **Cohen** Dennis |
| Michael **Cohen** | **Cohen** Michael |

7. Press the Home button to close the Display Order screen and return to the home screen.

8. Open the Contacts app.

   Your contacts appear in the sort order that you specified, with each contact appearing in the specified display order.

Set a default contacts account

On your iPad, you can have contact lists from a variety of sources: MobileMe, Google, Microsoft Exchange, and more. So what happens when you create a new contact on your iPad? Where does it go? You can specify that by setting a default contacts account.

Setting a default account for new contacts:

1. Tap Settings > Mail, Contacts, Calendars, and then, in the Mail, Contacts, Calendars screen, swipe down until you see the Contacts section.

2. Tap Default Account.

3. On the Default Account screen, tap the account into which you want your new contacts to go.

Set a calendar

Your iPad's Calendar app can display events from a lot of calendars. You can have a Home calendar, a Work calendar, a Holidays calendar, a Bills Due calendar, and more. Adding to the fun, the Calendar app can display calendars from several sources: those that come from your computer, those that you sync with MobileMe, those to which you subscribe, and so on. But on what calendar do the events that you create on your iPad go?

That's where the default calendar comes in. You can (and should) specify a default calendar so that when you create an event, you don't have to worry about what calendar will receive it. Unless you specify otherwise, newly created events end up in your default calendar.

 Although you can subscribe to and sync with a plethora of calendars from various sources, the iPad doesn't give you a way to create new calendars directly on it.

Setting a default calendar:

1. Tap Settings > Mail, Contacts, Calendars.

2. Swipe down the resulting Mail, Contacts, Calendars screen until you see the Calendars section, way down at the bottom.

3. Tap Default Calendar.

   The Default Calendar screen appears, listing some or all of the calendars displayed by your iPad's Calendar app (**Figure 1.26**).

 We say *some or all* because the iPad shows only the calendars to which you can add events. Subscribed calendars, for example, can't be altered, so they don't show up in the Default Calendar screen.

Figure 1.26 You can pick a default calendar from those on your iPad.

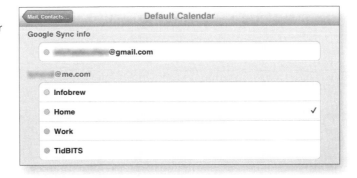

4. Tap the calendar that you want to use as your default.

   The next time you create an event in the Calendar app, the event is placed in your default calendar—that is, unless you choose another calendar for the event when you create it. For an example, see the Calendar setting in the Add Event dialog shown in **Figure 1.27**.

Figure 1.27 You can assign an event to a nondefault calendar when you create it.

note With iOS 4 or later, you can move an event to a different calendar on your iPad even after you create it.

Subscribe to a calendar

In the preceding section, we discuss calendars to which you subscribe. You may be wondering "What's *that* all about?" Here's what: Your iPad can display calendars that use the iCalendar format. Many people and organizations create calendars in that format and put them on the Web. If you like baseball, for example, you can find such calendars on the Major League Baseball site for your favorite teams. You can view such calendars, but you can't modify them.

Here, we show you how to subscribe to a Web-based calendar that presents daily history trivia as served up by a cartoon coffee bean. (Yes, the Web *is* stranger than you can imagine.)

Subscribing to a Web-based calendar:

1. Tap Safari, and go to http://homepage.mac.com/lymond/ infobrew.html.

    This Web page contains the most current pieces of coffee-flavored history trivia.

2. Scroll down to the bottom-left corner of the page, and tap the link titled Subscribe to Infobrew Calendar.

3. In the dialog that appears, tap Subscribe.

4. In the confirmation dialog, tap View Events.

    The Calendar app opens, and you can see the Infobrew calendar entries.

    If you don't want that calendar anymore (Infobrew, like coffee, is an acquired taste), getting rid of it is easy; just follow the next set of steps.

Removing a Web-based calendar subscription:

1. Tap Settings > Mail, Contacts, Calendars.

2. In the Accounts list, tap Subscribed Calendars.

3.　On the Calendars screen, tap the calendar you want to delete.

4.　At the bottom of the calendar information dialog that appears, tap Delete Account.

5.　In the Delete Account dialog that appears, tap Delete.

　　The calendar account is removed from your iPad, and its entries no longer appear in the Calendar app.

Hear calendar alerts

The calendar-alert settings are relatively minor—unless you miss an appointment or invitation because your iPad happened to be asleep at the critical time. The iPad has two sound-related settings that are associated with calendars: Calendar Alerts and New Invitation Alerts. When these settings are turned on, your iPad makes a sound when a calendar event is set and when one of your calendars receives a new invitation.

 Invitations go directly to one of your calendars in certain types of mail accounts, such as accounts on Microsoft Exchange servers.

Turning on alert sounds:

1.　Tap Settings > General > Sounds to open the Sounds screen.

2.　If the Calendar Alerts switch is off, tap it to turn it on.

3.　In the Settings pane on the left side of the screen, tap Mail, Contacts, Calendars.

4.　Swipe down the resulting Mail, Contacts, Calendars screen until you see the Calendars section at the bottom.

5.　If the New Invitation Alerts switch is off, tap it to turn it on.

　　From now on, whenever one of your calendars needs to alert you about an event or an invitation, your iPad makes a sound.

Use Time Zone Support

The Time Zone Support feature on your iPad seems to cause no end of confusion, if the number of posts on the Internet about it means anything. We'll try to clarify.

Your iPad has a Time Zone setting in its Date & Time settings pane. When you set your device for a different time zone, all the events in your calendars shift their times to accommodate that change.

Your iPad also has a Time Zone Support setting in its Calendar settings pane. When you turn that setting on and set a time zone, all the events in your calendars shift their times to match *that* time zone, regardless of what your iPad's Date & Time time-zone setting happens to be.

We imagine that you're still confused—enough so that you may have started drinking a little too early in the day. Put down that bottle. Here's a simple example that shows how you might use this confusing feature.

Suppose that you're traveling from Los Angeles to Boston via a connecting flight in Chicago. Your flight from Los Angeles leaves at 8 a.m. Pacific time. According to your flight itinerary, your connecting flight to Boston from Chicago leaves at 2 p.m. Central time. Here's what you do:

1. On your calendar, enter two events: your takeoff at 8 a.m. and your connecting flight at 2 p.m.

    (Yes, even though the second flight takes off at noon Los Angeles time, you don't need to do the math to figure that out.)

2. Turn on Time Zone Support, and set the time zone for Los Angeles.

3. Go catch your 8 a.m. flight out of LA.

4. When you land in Chicago, your iPad's clock is 2 hours off, so set your iPad's Date & Time time-zone setting to Chicago time.

    Now your iPad's clock is correct, but because you turned on Time Zone Support, the events in your calendars don't move. The departure time for your connecting flight is still 2 p.m. on your calendar, which is where you want it to be.

That's all there is to it. For everything to work properly, of course, your iPad needs to have its Date & Time setting properly set for Los Angeles when you start.

Setting the Date & Time time-zone setting:

1. Tap Settings > General to open the General settings screen.

2. Tap Date & Time to open the Date & Time screen.

3. Tap Time Zone to open the Time Zone screen.

4. In the search field at the top of the screen, begin to type the name of the closest big city in your time zone.

    A list of city names appears below the search field (**Figure 1.28**).

Figure 1.28 Pick a city in your time zone.

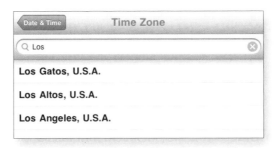

5. Tap a city that's in the same time zone as yours.

6. If necessary, tap the Date & Time arrow at the top of the screen to return to the Date & Time page, and set your iPad's clock to the current time.

Setting Time Zone Support:

1. Tap Settings > Mail, Contacts, Calendars.

2. Swipe down the resulting Mail, Contacts, Calendars screen until you see the Calendars section; then tap Time Zone Support.

    The Time Zone Support screen appears.

3. If the Time Zone Support switch is off, tap it to turn it on.

4. Tap Time Zone to open the Time Zone screen.

5. In the search field at the top of the screen, begin to type the name of a city in the time zone that you want.

    A list of cities appears below the search field.

6. Tap the city that's in the time zone you want.

    You're done!

Turn off Time Zone Support when you're not using it. If it's on and set for a different time zone from the one you're in, your calendar events may appear at the wrong times the next time you sync your iPad.

Get directions

This feature is a fun one to use and a real time-saver. In your Contacts app, every street address for each contact is linked to your iPad's Maps app. Here's how to use it.

Seeing a contact's address with the Maps app:

1. Open the Contacts app.

2. Choose a contact who has a street address.

3. Tap that street address.

    The Maps app opens, showing the location of the address you just tapped.

This feature is particularly helpful when you're traveling. Suppose that you're in a hotel, and you have a meeting with a client at her office. It's a simple matter to get directions from your hotel to your client's office. Read on.

Getting directions from your location to a contact's address:

1. In the Contacts app, tap a contact's address.

    The Maps app opens, with your contact's address pinpointed on the map and the address displayed in the search field in the top-right corner.

2. Tap the Directions button in the top-left corner of the map.

    The contact's address appears in the rightmost field at the top of the map, which is the Destination field. In most cases, your current location appears in the Start field.

3. If your current location doesn't appear in the Start field, tap the Start field and then choose Current Location from the Recents list.

A blue line highlights the route on the map from your current location to the destination. At the bottom of the screen is a blue panel
that offers you detailed instructions for getting there by walking,
driving, or taking public transportation (**Figure 1.29**).

Figure 1.29 You can
get there from here—
just tap Start and fol-
low the directions.

4. In the blue panel, tap the icon for the method of transportation you
   prefer, and then tap Start.

   A step-by-step list of instructions for getting to the destination appears.

iPad Protection Project

Difficulty level: Easy

Software needed: MobileMe account (optional)

iPad model: Any

Additional hardware: None

In the 1976 film *Marathon Man,* the malevolent Dr. Christian Szell asks the protagonist, "Is it safe?" If he'd been asking about your iPad, the answer would have to be "Probably not."

As configured right out of the box, the iPad is open to anyone. Pick it up, press the Sleep/Wake button, and drag the onscreen slider to the right—or, even easier, just flip open the Smart Cover on an iPad 2—and all your iPad's secrets are revealed. Naturally, this revelation isn't much of a problem if you live alone and your iPad stays at home with you. (Trust us—your cat doesn't care what's on your iPad.) But the iPad is a very portable object, and an attractive one, too; it cries out to be picked up, tried out, played with. If you leave it lying around, someone—even someone you know, trust, and love—can easily find it irresistible.

There isn't any way to make the iPad completely impervious to prying eyes. A knowledgeable person with enough time and the right software can crack almost any security scheme. Nonetheless, you can protect your iPad's contents from the casual snooper and even give determined data thieves pause.

Also, if you share your iPad with your children from time to time (it's a great way to keep kids entertained on long car trips, for example), you can protect them from content that might be too mature for young eyes and ears.

Finally, you can even have the iPad tell you where it is if you misplace it (easy to do; these things love to hide under magazines and pillows) or if someone "accidentally" wanders off with it.

Fasten the passcode lock

The iPad has a built-in passcode lock that you can use to halt snoopers dead in their tracks when they wake it up. As soon as a snooper slides the Slide to Unlock slider or opens the Smart Cover, he's greeted by a dialog demanding a passcode. Without that passcode, all the snooper can see is your Lock Screen wallpaper. You can choose a simple passcode that consists of a four-digit number (easy to remember, time-consuming to crack) or a longer passcode that combines letters, numbers, and punctuation (even safer, but harder to remember and to type). Which kind of passcode you choose depends on just how much trouble you want to give a snooper.

note

When you set a passcode, all versions of iOS 4 encrypt the data on your iPad, making your information much harder to steal, even for sophisticated data thieves. If you've upgraded an original iPad from iOS 3, however, the encryption may not be complete. Apple has provided instructions for encrypting all the data on such iPads; see "iOS 4: Understanding data protection" at http://support.apple.com/kb/HT4175.

Setting a passcode:

1. On the home screen, tap the Settings app's icon.

2. On the left side of the Settings screen, tap General.

3. On the right side of the resulting General screen, tap Passcode Lock.

    The Passcode Lock screen appears (**Figure 1.30**).

Figure 1.30 Use the Passcode Lock screen to set a passcode and decide what kind of passcode to use.

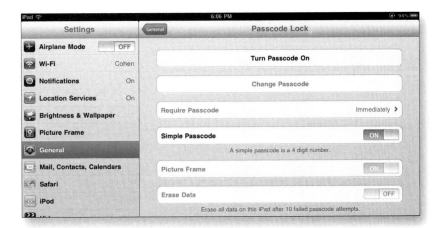

4. (Optional) Tap the Simple Passcode switch to turn it off if you want to use a longer, safer passcode that combines letters, numbers, and punctuation.

5. Tap Turn Passcode On.

   The Set Passcode dialog appears (**Figure 1.31**). If you chose to turn off Simple Passcode in Step 4, the onscreen keyboard also appears so that you can type a complicated passcode.

Figure 1.31 Set either a simple four-digit pass-code (left) or a longer, safer one (right).

6. Enter the passcode of your choosing and then repeat it when you're asked to confirm the passcode.

   As soon as you enter the passcode, the passcode lock takes effect. By default, the next time you put your iPad to sleep and then wake it up, you must enter the passcode in the Passcode Lock screen—even if you put the device to sleep for only a few seconds. You can change how long the iPad has to be asleep before the passcode lock takes effect, however.

 If you want to use your iPad's picture-frame feature when you have a passcode enabled, tap the Picture Frame switch on the Passcode Lock screen to turn it on.

Choose a Good Passcode

Choose a passcode that you can remember easily but that's hard for other people to guess. Try these tips:

- If you use a simple passcode, avoid making that code something like your birthday. Instead, choose something less obvious that you can remember, such as the third through sixth digits of your phone number when you were in high school (and no, that's not the simple passcode we use, but thanks for playing!).

- For longer passcodes, a two-word phrase with numbers and punctuation between the words, such as *land*32*shark*, can be easy to remember but hard to guess (and, no, we don't use that one, either!).

Changing the passcode-lock interval:

1. In the Passcode Lock screen (see the preceding section), tap Require Passcode.

2. In the Require Passcode screen, tap the length of time you want to elapse before the lock kicks in.

   As the screen points out, shorter intervals are safer.

3. (Optional) At the top of the Require Passcode screen, tap Passcode Lock; then, in the Passcode Lock screen, tap the Erase Data switch to turn it on.

   This feature guards your iPad against those who might abscond with it and then try passcode after passcode to unlock it. After ten attempts, your iPad is erased, so the thief has only your valuable iPad, not the possibly even more valuable data that it contains.

tip **If you manage to erase your data accidentally, you can recover it from the automatic backup that iTunes creates each time you sync your iPad with iTunes—another good reason to sync with iTunes periodically, even if you normally sync your information wirelessly. See the Apple article at http://support.apple.com/kb/HT1414 for details on restoring your iPad.**

Think of the children—and the adults

As we mention earlier in this project, the iPad is a wonderful child-distraction device. Even pudgy toddler fingers can manage to tap their way around it. But your iPad may contain some items—such as movies, songs, or TV shows—that you really don't want your toddler to see. Neither do you want your 9-year-old daughter wandering into the iTunes Store and buying a few hundred dollars' worth of tunes to die for. For that matter, if you share your iPad with anyone, child or adult, you may want to make sure that this person won't mess up your mail-account settings or inadvertently add a few dozen "friends" to any multiplayer games you may enjoy.

You can set restrictions to guard against the accidental viewing of certain media or the semiaccidental use of certain apps.

Setting up restrictions:

1. Tap Settings > General > Restrictions to open the Restrictions screen.

2. At the top of the screen, tap Enable Restrictions.

   A passcode dialog appears, similar to the one you use to set simple passcodes (refer to Figure 1.31 earlier in this project).

3. Tap out a four-digit passcode of your choosing and then repeat it to confirm the passcode.

 This passcode can be the same as your simple passcode (refer to "Setting a passcode" earlier in this project), but for better security, you should choose a different one.

   After you establish the passcode, the rest of the choices in this screen become available. With them, you can disallow access to certain apps and features, as well as restrict access to certain types of media based on parental ratings (**Figure 1.32**).

Figure 1.32 Restrict access to various apps, actions, and types of content here.

4. Set your restrictions:

   - **Purchases, privacy, and Web surfing.** In the Allow section, for example, you can make the iTunes Store inaccessible, so that guest users can't buy music or video; you can block the installation or deletion of apps; and you can hide the built-in YouTube and Safari apps to keep young, inquisitive eyes from gazing on some of the Internet's seamier sights. If you have an iPad 2, you can also disable the cameras and block the use of FaceTime (useful if you share your iPad with hormonally overloaded adolescents).

note Disabling Safari doesn't guarantee that iPad users can't get onto the Web; many apps contain built-in browsers that continue to work even when Safari is disabled.

- **Location and accounts.** If you're worried that your iPad might violate your privacy by reporting your current location to a third party, you can tap Location in the Allow Changes section to specify which apps can (and can't) use the iPad's Location Services feature, and after you've chosen a set of apps that can use Location Services, you can lock down those settings. To protect your current Mail, Calendar, and Contact account settings, you can tap Accounts in the Allow Changes section.

- **In-app purchases.** You can further protect your pocketbook by turning off In-App Purchases in the Allowed Content section.

- **Movies and TV shows.** In the same Allowed Content section, you can tap Ratings For to specify the national ratings system that the iPad uses when you restrict access to movies and TV shows. You can restrict movie viewing to G and PG movies when the ratings are set for the United States, for example. Switch the Ratings For setting to France instead, and you can restrict movies by the age-level ratings used in that country.

- **Explicit songs and apps.** You can ban music with explicit lyrics as listed in the iTunes Store, and you can hide apps that have age restrictions as listed in the App Store.

- **Games.** The iPad's Game Center allows you to participate in multiplayer games and add friends to your gaming environment. You can disable either action in the Game Center section of the Restrictions screen.

 This system isn't perfect. Determined children (and childlike adults) can find their way around seemingly impervious obstacles, so you still need to exercise some oversight. But the available restriction options do go a long way toward making your iPad more child-friendly and sharable.

Search and recover with Find My iPad

Lost may have been great TV entertainment, but it's not so entertaining when it's your precious iPad that's lost. By using MobileMe's Find My iPad feature, however, you may be able to find your lost device and rescue it from the island. Even if you can't rescue it, you can still use the Find My iPad feature to lock your iPad with a new passcode or even wipe out its contents so that your information can't be hijacked and misused.

You don't need a MobileMe account to use the Find My iPad feature, however. All you need is a free Apple ID. Getting an Apple ID is easy, and when you have one (or if you *do* have a MobileMe account), activating Find My iPad takes just a few taps.

Getting a free Apple ID:

1. Tap Settings > Mail, Contacts, Calendars.

2. At the bottom of the Accounts list on the right side of the screen, tap Add Account, and then, in the Add Accounts pane, tap MobileMe.

    The MobileMe dialog appears (**Figure 1.33**).

Figure 1.33 Create a free Apple ID via MobileMe.

3. Tap Create Free Apple ID.

    A series of New Apple ID dialogs appears, requesting information like the country where you're located, your date of birth, and—most important—an email account that will serve as your Apple ID.

4. Supply the information requested in each of the New Apple ID dialogs, tapping Next as you finish filling out each one.

    After you supply the required information, you're asked to agree to the MobileMe terms of service.

5. Read the terms of service and then tap Agree.

    Naturally, if you don't agree, you can't use the service.

After you agree, Apple sends a verification email to the email address you specified in Step 4. If you've already set up a mail account on your iPad for that email address, you can open the verification email on your iPad; otherwise, you should be at a computer that can receive email for that address.

6. In the verification email that Apple sends you, click the link to verify the account.

   If you received the email on a computer, your Web browser opens to a page where you can sign in to MobileMe with your Apple ID and password. On your iPad, you see a sign-in screen.

7. Sign in with your Apple ID and password to complete the account-creation process.

Enabling Find My iPad:

1. Tap Settings > Mail, Contacts, Calendars.

2. In the list of accounts on the right side of the Mail, Contacts, Calendars screen, tap your MobileMe account.

   An account-settings dialog appears (**Figure 1.34**).

Figure 1.34 Find My iPad is linked to your MobileMe account, whether that account is one you pay for or is associated with a free Apple ID.

3. Tap the Find My iPad to switch to set it to On.

4. Tap the blue Done button in the top-right corner.

   Now that Find My iPad is activated, you can ask Apple to locate your device for you, which it can do as long as (a) your iPad is awake, (b) your iPad is sleeping within range of a Wi-Fi network connected to the Internet, or (c) your 3G iPad is within range of the mobile-phone network.

tip   **You can also ask Apple to find your iPad with its Find My iPhone service, which works with iPhones, iPod touches, and iPads. You can use this service in a Web browser, or you can download and use the free Find My iPhone app from the App Store.**

Finding your iPad with a Web browser:

1. Go to www.me.com, and sign in with your MobileMe ID or Apple ID and its associated password.

   If you have a free Apple ID, a map appears after a few moments, pinpointing your iPad's current whereabouts. You can skip to step 4.

   If you have a paid MobileMe account, however, you need to complete the next two steps.

note   **The Find My iPhone app works very much like the Web service. You enter your MobileMe information and then use a map interface almost identical to the one in the Web version.**

2. Click the cloud symbol in the top-left corner of the browser window and then click Find My iPhone.

3. Enter your MobileMe password again.

   The map appears, with your iPad pinpointed on it.

4. Decide what to do about your iPad.

   When you click your iPad's location on the map (**Figure 1.35** on the next page), you can choose to have your iPad display a message and play a sound for 2 minutes (useful if you've misplaced your iPad around the house; just listen for the sound to track the wandering iPad down).

Figure 1.35 Choose what to do with the iPad that MobileMe found.

If, however, your iPad is in some strange, unanticipated place, in the grasp of some foul iPad-snatcher, you can set a new passcode for your iPad (to prevent the evildoer from accessing your information easily) or even erase the information on your iPad (if you suspect that the evildoer is particularly nefarious and dastardly). See "Fasten the passcode lock" earlier in this project for details.

> **tip** **If you do choose to wipe your iPad's information and are fortunate enough to recover the device later, you can use the Restore feature to put the most recent backup of your information back on your iPad. See http://support.apple.com/kb/HT1414 for more information about restoring your iPad. This tip also works if you have to obtain a replacement iPad instead.**

Weave a Wiki Project

Difficulty level: Intermediate

Software needed: Trunk Notes 2.4.3 ($3.99)

Optional software: TextExpander touch app ($4.99), Dropbox (free)

iPad model: Any

Additional hardware: None

A *wiki* is a Web site that allows you to create and edit any number of inter-linked Web pages or documents via a Web browser, using a simplified markup language called *Markdown* to control formatting, layout, and linking. Wikis were invented by programmer Ward Cunningham, who described a wiki as "the simplest online database that could possibly work."

The name wiki is derived from the Hawaiian word wikiwiki, which means quick.

Wikis are often used to share information, organize notes, and create collaborative works such as the best-known wiki: Wikipedia (http://en.wikipedia.org/wiki/Main_Page).

The Trunk Notes app, which you use in this project, gives you an efficient, simple way to organize documents and information—such as shopping lists, lists of books you want to read, recipes, and class notes—in the form of wiki pages.

Work with Trunk Notes

Before you start creating your own Trunk Notes wiki, you need to know how to browse and search Trunk Notes.

 Trunk Notes is *modal,* which means that whenever you use it, you're always in one of three modes: browse, edit, or search mode. If you're in browse mode, you see an Edit button to the right of the Search field and a Home button in the bottom-left corner of the screen. If you're in edit mode, you see a Save button to the right of the Search field. Finally, if you're in search mode, you see a Cancel button to the right of the Search field.

Viewing Trunk Notes:

1. Launch the Trunk Notes app by tapping its icon.

    You see the default home page (**Figure 1.36**).

Figure 1.36 Trunk Notes Home page.

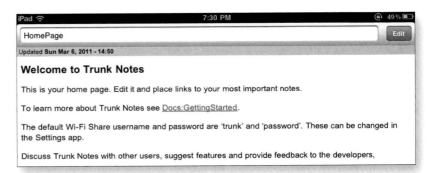

The Search field at the top of the screen displays the name of the current entry as a wikiword.

A *wikiword* is two or more words joined together without spaces and with each word beginning with a capital letter, like this: *WikiWord*.

The second sentence from the top of the home page reads *To learn more about Trunk Notes see Docs:GettingStarted.* The words *Docs:GettingStarted* are in blue and underlined to indicate that they link to a page or entry in Trunk Notes.

2. Tap the Docs:GettingStarted hyperlink.

You're taken to the Getting Started page (**Figure 1.37**).

Figure 1.37 Getting Started page.

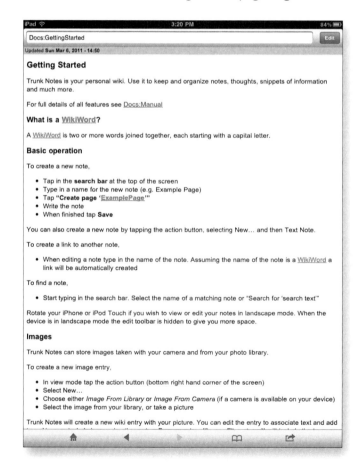

At the bottom of the Getting Started page is the navigation bar (**Figure 1.38**)—a row of small icons used for wiki navigation.

Figure 1.38 Trunk Notes navigation bar.

Here's how you use the navigation-bar icons:

- The Home icon, which looks like a small house, returns you to the home page from any page you're browsing.

- The Back and Forward icons allow you to navigate your wiki based on your navigation history. Tapping the left triangle takes you to the preceding page in your Trunk Notes browsing history; tapping the right triangle takes you to the next page in your history. A triangle is grayed out if you don't yet have any entries for that direction in your Trunk Notes history.

- The Bookmark icon displays a popover listing all the existing pages in your wiki, as shown in **Figure 1.39** (though you won't have the same pages). The buttons at the bottom of the popover allow you to display wiki entries sorted alphabetically by name, by age (Today, Yesterday, This Month, Earlier), and by popularity.

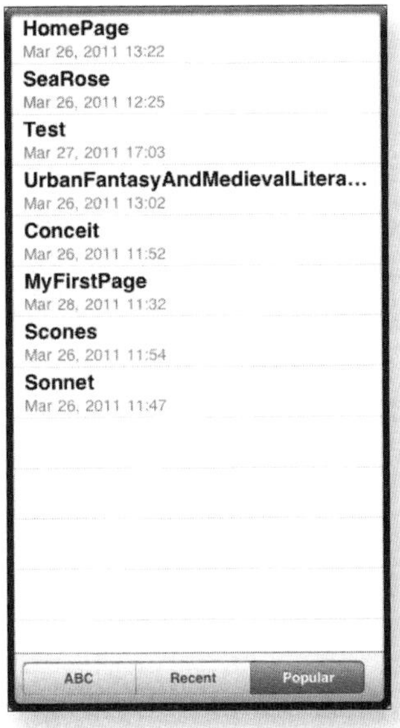

Figure 1.39 Wiki pages.

HomePage
Mar 26, 2011 13:22
SeaRose
Mar 26, 2011 12:25
Test
Mar 27, 2011 17:03
UrbanFantasyAndMedievalLitera...
Mar 26, 2011 13:02
Conceit
Mar 26, 2011 11:52
MyFirstPage
Mar 28, 2011 11:32
Scones
Mar 26, 2011 11:54
Sonnet
Mar 26, 2011 11:47

| ABC | Recent | Popular |

- Tapping the curved-arrow Action icon while you're in browse mode displays a popover that lists the following options:

  - *New.* This option allows you to create an image-only page by selecting an image from the Photos app or (on an iPad 2) to photograph a new image and create a page for it.

  - *Duplicate.* This option copies the current page and lets you give the copy a new name.

 Choose Duplicate to create a template containing text and images that you want to use on more than one page. You could create a note-taking template, for example, that has areas for a summary, important points, or a to-do list.

  - *Wi-Fi Sharing.* For details on this option, see "Share your wiki" later in this project.

  - *Mail.* Tapping Mail displays a second popover, providing the options Mail Entry, Mail Entry As Text, and Mail Backup. Mail Entry emails a formatted copy of the page to an address you supply. Mail Entry As Text sends a copy of the page in Markdown syntax. Mail Backup sends a zipped backup of your entire wiki (the current version doesn't include images) to an email address you supply. Depending on the size of your wiki, compiling the pages and zipping them could take a while.

  - *Dropbox Sync.* This option allows you to sync your entire wiki (via the free Dropbox app) on other iOS devices or your computer.

 You see these options again in "Sharing over Wi-Fi" at the end of this project.

Searching Trunk Notes:

1. If Trunk Notes isn't open, tap the Trunk Notes icon to launch the app.

2. If you aren't on the home page (refer to Figure 1.36 earlier in this project), tap the Home icon in the navigation bar at the bottom of the page.

3. Do one of the following things:

   - If you're in edit mode, tap the Save button in the top-right corner of the screen.

   - If you're in search mode, tap the Cancel button in the top-right corner of the screen.

4. Tap inside the Search field at the top of the screen, and type (exactly as printed here) **Docs:GettingStarted**.

   As soon as you start typing, the existing text in the Search field (probably the name of the Trunk Notes page you were on when you started typing) is replaced by the text you're entering, because now you're now in search mode.

   Before you finish typing, Trunk Notes displays a list of options on a screen that resembles lined paper (**Figure 1.40**).

Figure 1.40 Search-results screen.

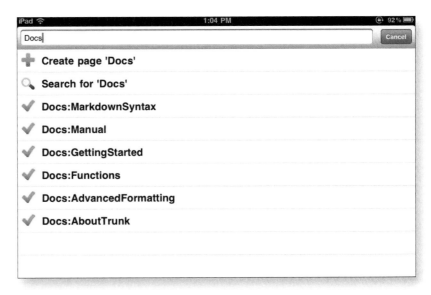

The second line has a magnifying glass to its left. Tap that icon to search for the text you entered in the body of all the Trunk Notes pages.

The remaining lines have a green check to their left, which means that those lines represent Trunk Notes entries or pages that already exist. One of the pages in the list should be Docs:GettingStarted.

> **tip** In later searches, you may see a blue tag icon to the left of one or more words in this list. Tap a tag result to see a list of pages that were tagged with that word.

5. Tap Docs:GettingStarted.

Trunk Notes displays the Getting Started page (refer to Figure 1.37 earlier in this project).

Now you can find the Getting Started page any time you need help. This page contains links to other help pages and to the Trunk Notes manual.

Create Trunk Notes pages

Trunk Notes pages or entries (both terms are accurate) can be about anything you want. They can contain images, text, links to other Trunk Notes pages or to the Web, or even sound that you record with Trunk Notes.

You can create pages at any time without having to create their contents; you can always go back later to edit pages.

Creating a wiki entry:

1. To create a new page, tap inside the Search field at the top of the Trunk Notes window (refer to Figure 1.36 earlier in this project).

2. Type (exactly as printed here) **MyFirstEntry** in the Search field.

As you begin to type, the existing text in the field disappears, and you see a new page that resembles lined paper (**Figure 1.41**). The first line displays a green plus sign next to Create page 'MyFirstEntry', and the second line displays a magnifying glass next to Search for 'My First Entry'.

Figure 1.41 The Create Page screen.

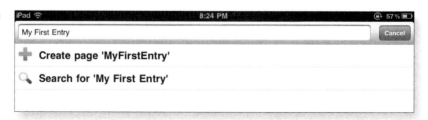

3. Tap the first line (the one with the green plus sign).

    You see a new page in edit mode (**Figure 1.42**). You know that you're in edit mode because you see a Save button in the top-right corner of the screen. The title of the page is in the Search field. Below that is a large blank body-text area, ready for you to type.

Figure 1.42 A blank MyFirstEntry page, ready for your text.

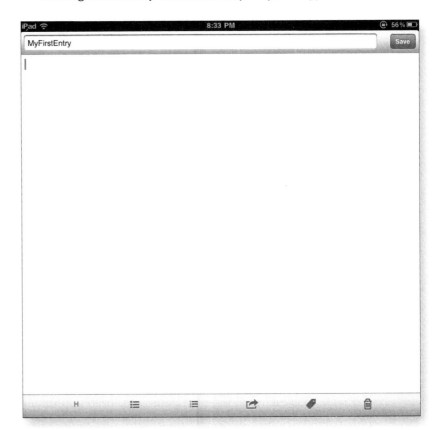

4. Enter some text.

    For now, it doesn't matter what you type, because you're going to delete it later.

5. When you've entered a line or two, tap the Save button.

    You'll see something like **Figure 1.43** (on the next page), though your text will probably be different.

Figure 1.43
MyFirstEntry, with text
in the body of the page.

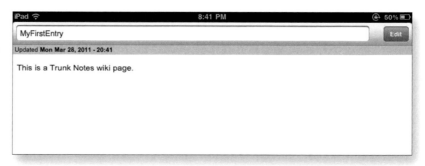

 You can't create or edit notes containing wikiwords that start with
Docs:, *Special:*, or *New:*.

Format wiki text

Trunk Notes uses Markdown syntax for formatting (see the sidebar
"Markdown Syntax" later in this section), because it's an easy way to
format text by using simple codes. But you'll usually use the formatting
buttons at the bottom of edit screens for most of your formatting. If you
know HTML, you can also use most HTML tags in Trunk Notes pages.

Formatting text in Trunk Notes:

1. If Trunk Notes isn't open, open it by tapping the Trunk Notes icon.

2. If the app doesn't open to the MyFirstEntry page, search for
    MyFirstEntry (see "Searching Trunk Notes" earlier in this project).

3. Tap the Edit button in the top-left corner of the MyFirstEntry page.

    You're in edit mode. At the bottom of the screen is a row of formatting
    buttons (**Figure 1.44**). These buttons insert Markdown codes that tell
    Trunk Notes how to format your text.

	Bulleted	*Numbered*			
Heading	*List*	*List*	*Action*	*Tag*	*Trash*

Figure 1.44
Formatting-bar
buttons.

 You can read more about Markdown in the Trunk Notes online manual
at www.appsonthemove.com/Docs_MarkdownSyntax.html.

Here's how you use the formatting-bar buttons:

- Tapping the Heading button (H) creates a heading. You can have up to five levels of subheads by tapping the Heading button up to five more times before entering the heading text. The headings get smaller with each additional level.

- Tapping the Bulleted List or Numbered List button once creates a list; tapping either button a second time creates a nested list. When you finish adding items to a list, insert two returns (using the iPad's digital keyboard or a Bluetooth keyboard) to indicate the end of one paragraph and the start of another.

- Tapping the Action button displays a popover of options for the entry, including Clear Text, Insert Timestamp, Insert Link To, Insert, Encrypt, and Update Geotag.

- Tapping the Tag button tags an entry with descriptive keywords called *tags*. When you tap Tag, you can enter a new tag or search for words you've used before as tags; Trunk Notes displays a list of all the entries that have those tags.

- Tapping the Trash button deletes the current entry.

 If you delete an entry, you can't recover it.

4. Tap the Action button at the bottom of the screen.

   You see a popover like the one shown in **Figure 1.45**.

Figure 1.45
Action-button popover.

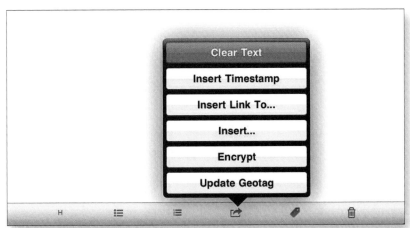

5. Tap the red Clear Text button to clear all your text from MyFirstPage.

6. Tap the Heading button at the bottom of the screen.

   This button inserts a pound sign (#) followed by a space and tells Trunk Notes to format the following text as a heading when you save.

7. Type **Shopping List** after the # and the space, and tap the Return key on your iPad keyboard to start a new line.

8. Tap the Bulleted List button at the bottom of the screen.

   Trunk Notes inserts the Markdown code for a bulleted-list item: an asterisk (*) followed by a space.

9. Type **Milk**, and tap the Return key.

10. Type **Bread**, and tap the Return key.

11. Tap the Save button.

    Your screen should look something like **Figure 1.46**.

Figure 1.46
A bulleted list.

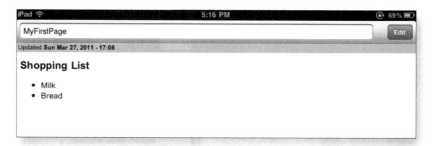

12. Tap the Edit button in the top-right corner of the screen.

    Your cursor should be right after the *d* in *Bread*.

13. Tap Return on the iPad's digital keyboard and then tap the Bulleted List button at the bottom of the screen.

14. Type **Whole wheat** and then tap the Save button.

    You've made an indented list—a list with a sublist—that should look something like **Figure 1.47**.

Figure 1.47 A bulleted list with a sublist.

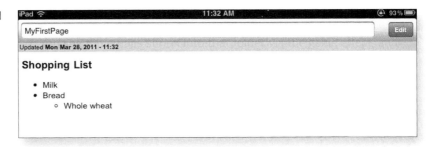

 The TextExpander touch app, from Smile software, allows you to create snippets of reusable text and use them in any app that allows you to paste. In apps like Trunk Notes that support TextExpander touch, you can invoke TextExpander touch from within the app and save yourself a considerable amount of typing.

Markdown Syntax

Markdown is a method of inserting simple codes for formatting documents. You can also use most HTML codes, if you know HTML, but Markdown is much faster in terms of typing on an iPad.

The codes for Markdown are very simple:

- **Paragraphs:** Insert a blank line by tapping the Return key on the iPad's digital keyboard. Make sure that there isn't a leading space at the beginning of the blank line.

- **Headings:** Type # at the beginning of a line to create a first-level heading, ## at the beginning of a line for a second-level heading, and so on, up to six levels of headings.

- **Bold text:** Type ** before the text you want to be bold and ** at the end of that text to turn off the bold formatting.

- **Italic text:** Type * before the text you want to italicize and * at the end of that text to turn off the italics.

- **Bulleted lists:** Begin each list item with a space followed by an asterisk (*).

- **Numbered lists:** Begin each list item with a space, followed by a number and then a period (**1.**). The number doesn't matter; Trunk Notes automatically numbers list items based on their order.

Markdown codes don't appear onscreen in Trunk Notes when you aren't in edit mode. Trunk Notes converts the codes to formatted text when you save an entry.

Adding internal links to Trunk Notes pages:

1. Open Trunk Notes to its home page.

2. Tap inside the Search field, and type **EntryWithLinks**.

3. On the search-results screen, tap Create page 'EntryWithLinks'.

4. Tap the Action button at the bottom of the screen.

    A popover appears (refer to Figure 1.45 earlier in this project).

5. Tap Insert Link To in the popover.

    A list of Trunk Notes entries appears.

6. Tap MyFirstPage.

    Trunk Notes inserts [[MyFirstPage]], as shown in **Figure 1.48**. The double brackets around a wikiword are Markdown code for a Trunk Notes page.

Figure 1.48 A page showing the Markdown code for an internal link.

Typing a wikiword in the body of a Trunk Notes page automatically creates a link that goes to a new blank entry or page if no such page exists, and if the page exists, typing the wikiword name for that page creates a link to the page.

7. Tap the Save button.

    Your page should look similar to **Figure 1.49**. The phrase *MyFirstPage* is now a hyperlink; tap it to go to that entry.

Figure 1.49 A page showing a hyperlink.

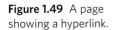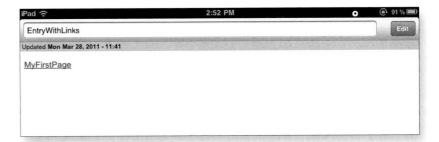

tip

You can create a link to a Web page that will open in Safari by formatting the link this way: Put the link text in square brackets and the actual URL in parentheses, like this:

[*Example link*](*http://www.example.com*).

Adding an image to a Trunk Notes page:

1. Open Trunk Notes to its home page.

2. Tap inside the Search field, and type **MyImageEntry**.

3. In the resulting edit page, tap Create page 'MyImageEntry'.

4. Tap the Action button at the bottom of the screen to display a popover.

5. Choose Insert from the popover.

A new popover appears (**Figure 1.50**).

Figure 1.50 The Insert popover.

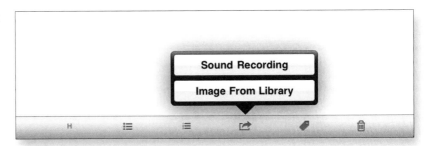

6. Tap Image From Library.

   Another new popover opens, listing the albums in your Photos app. Your albums will be different, but the list will look something like **Figure 1.51**.

Figure 1.51 The Photo Albums popover.

7. Tap an album to select it.

8. Tap the thumbnail of the image you want to use in your MyImageEntry page.

   Trunk Notes inserts Markdown syntax that will display your image when you tap Save. This code looks something like **Figure 1.52**.

Figure 1.52 A page showing Markdown syntax for an image.

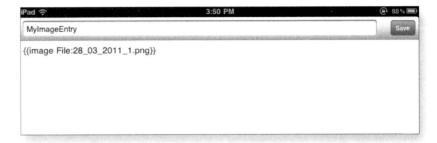

9. Tap the Save button in the top-right corner of the screen.

   Your entry will have a different image, of course, but should look similar to **Figure 1.53**.

Figure 1.53 Trunk Notes page with an image.

Share your wiki

If you share your Trunk Notes wiki on your iPad over a local Wi-Fi connection, you can browse, edit, and search for your wiki pages on your computer by using a Web browser. First, however, you need to configure Trunk Notes settings on your iPad to allow sharing.

Configuring Trunk Notes for sharing:

1. Tap the Settings icon on your iPad to open the Settings screen.

2. Scroll down to tap Trunk Notes in the Apps category (**Figure 1.54**).

Figure 1.54 The Trunk Notes panel in iPad Settings.

3. In the Wi-Fi Sharing section at the bottom of the screen, make sure that the Authentication switch is set to On.

4. Change the Username entry from the default setting (trunk).

5. Change the password from the default password to something that you'll remember easily.

6. Unless you have a good reason to change the Port setting, leave it at its default setting (10000), which is part of the address Trunk Notes will use for sharing your wiki.

The Don't Fall Asleep setting means that the Wi-Fi connection between your iPad and computer will be kept live. Instead of running down the iPad's battery, you may want to leave Don't Fall Asleep turned off. If your iPad falls asleep, you need to wake it again by touching the screen.

Sharing over Wi-Fi:

1. Open Trunk Notes to its home page.

2. Tap the Action button at the bottom of the screen.

   A popover appears (**Figure 1.55**).

Figure 1.55 The navigation bar's Action-button popover.

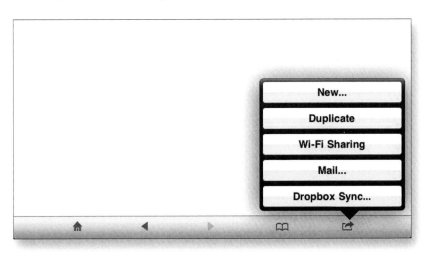

3. From the popover, choose Wi-Fi Sharing.

   You see a Wi-Fi Sharing window similar to the one shown in **Figure 1.56**. This window displays a URL for you to enter in a Web browser on your computer; this URL may differ from one time to another.

Figure 1.56 The Wi-Fi Sharing window.

4. Enter the URL from this window in the address field of a Web browser on your computer.

The text can't be copied; you need to type it.

5. Tap the blue Done button in the top-left corner of the Wi-Fi Sharing window on your iPad.

6. On your computer, go to the address you entered in your Web browser.

    You should see the Trunk Notes home page (**Figure 1.57**), where you can browse your Trunk Notes pages, edit them, or create new ones.

Figure 1.57 The Trunk Notes home page, viewed in a Web browser.

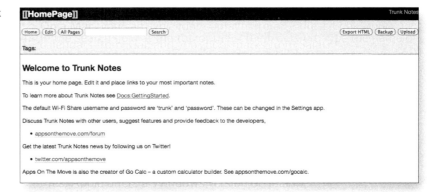

> **tip** Click the All Pages button at the top of the home page to see a list of all your Trunk Notes pages.

Any changes you make will be saved to your iPad when you click the Save button in your Web browser (**Figure 1.58**).

Figure 1.58 The edit screen in a Web browser.

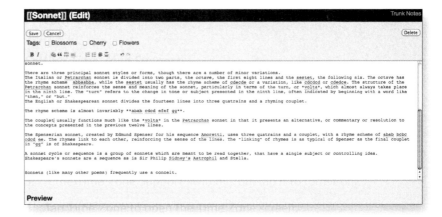

Now What?

You can do a lot more with Trunk Notes, which has many other features we haven't even mentioned, such as these:

- You can insert a date-and-time stamp and record audio, for example, which makes Trunk Notes ideal for taking notes in class or at a meeting.

- You can use Dropbox to sync, share, and edit Trunk Notes pages from your iPhone and other iOS devices.

- You can make sure that private notes stay private by encrypting them with Trunk Notes' built-in AES-256 encryption.

For more information, take a look at the online Trunk Notes manual at www.appsonthemove.com/manual.html.

2

Working and Playing in the iPad

When the iPad made its debut in 2010, the conventional wisdom branded it as just a media-consumption device, and the conventional wisdom was right...except for that four-letter word *just*.

In this chapter, we show you how to do more with your iPad. Turn the page and follow along as we demonstrate how to get real work done with it: in the kitchen, in the classroom, in the office, on the Web. In case you get exhausted by all that work, we also show you how to plan a vacation with the iPad.

Why do we do all this? We do it because the iPad is more than just a media-consumption device. That's *our* unconventional wisdom.

Go to Meeting Project

Difficulty level: Easy

Software needed: iTunes 10.2 or later, Dropbox 1.3.1 (free), GoodReader 3.5 ($4.99), Instapaper 3.0.1 ($4.99)

iPad model: Any

Additional hardware: None

Your iPad is fabulous, and you take it just about everywhere you go. Why not use it for work, in or out of the office? This project talks about moving files back and forth among your iPad, your computer, your colleagues, and the 'net. We show you how to download and read files via email, iTunes, and Dropbox; how to read and mark up a PDF in GoodReader; and how to use Instapaper to mark Web content for later reading.

Email files to yourself

Probably the easiest way to move a file between your computer and your iPad (or smartphone) is to send the file as an email attachment. You create the email on your computer and attach the file you want to be able to use on your iPad. Then you send the file to yourself, using an address in a mail account that you can access on your iPad. Mail on the iPad can preview PDFs; iWork files; and Microsoft Word, Excel, and PowerPoint files.

There's a catch, however: The iPad can preview only certain file formats (see the nearby sidebar "Mail Attachments That the iPad Can Preview"). You can view these files in Mail—or see them or hear them—but you can't edit them in Mail. If you want to modify or edit these files, you need another app. We describe some of the ways to edit files later in this project.

If you do have an app that can edit a file type, Mail may know about it and ask whether you want to open the attached file in that app—another task that we cover later in this project.

 If Mail or the iPad doesn't support the format of an attached file, you see the name of the attached file in the body of the email, but you can't open it on your iPad. You may be able to open it on a computer, however.

Emailing yourself a file to preview on the iPad:

1. Using a computer instead of your iPad, address an email to yourself.

    Be sure to use an address in an email account that you've set up on your iPad (see the **Mail Management Project** in Chapter 1). Fill out the Subject line, too, so that your Internet service provider won't think it's spam.

2. Attach a file that you want to read on your iPad.

    For the purposes of this task and the next one, attach a Microsoft Word .doc file.

 The process for previewing other kinds of files on your iPad is very similar. The "Mail Attachments That the iPad Can Preview" sidebar lists files that the iPad and Mail can read natively.

3. Send the email to yourself.

Mail Attachments That the iPad Can Preview

By *preview,* Apple means that you can view, read, or play the following file formats within Mail. You can't edit previewed files, though you may be able to use the Copy command.

- **Adobe Acrobat and Preview (Mac) files:** .pdf

- **ASCII/text files:** .txt

- **Audio files:** .aac, .aiff, .mp3, and .wav (all of which you can play in the Mail app)

- **Image files:** .gif, .jpg, and .tiff (displayed as inline images in Mail)

- **iWork files:** .key (Keynote), .numbers (Numbers), and .pages (Pages)

- **Microsoft Office files:** .doc and .docx (Word), .ppt and .pptx (PowerPoint), and .xls and .xlsx (Excel)

- **Rich-text files:** .rtf

- **vCard files:** .vcf (which you can import into Contacts; see the **Mail Management Project** in Chapter 1)

- **Web pages:** .htm and .html

Previewing a Microsoft Word file in Mail:

1. Open an email with an attached Word file (see the preceding task).

You see an icon in the body of the email like the one shown in **Figure 2.1**. (If you've installed another app that can read Word files on the iPad, you may see that app's icon instead.)

Figure 2.1 Icon for an attached Word file in Mail.

2. Tap the icon.

A preview screen opens (**Figure 2.2**).

Figure 2.2 Mail showing a preview of a Word document.

3. Read the document.

    If the attached file is a multiple-page document, you can swipe up or down to page through the file. You can copy and paste from the previewed document, though you can't edit it.

4. When you finish reading, tap the blue Done button in the top-left corner.

    The preview screen disappears, and the email you began with is revealed.

If you tap the curved-arrow Action button in the top-right corner of a Mail preview screen, you see a popover like the one in Figure 2.3.

Figure 2.3 Open in popover.

Use Dropbox to share and sync files

Dropbox allows you to share data between computers and other devices by storing your files on its servers. A free account gives you 2 GB of file storage. (You'll be warned before you reach the limit.) You can access any files that you upload from any device that has Dropbox installed or from the Dropbox Web site:

*   **On your computer,** Dropbox creates a Dropbox folder. Any file or folder that you add to the Dropbox folder is available to you via Dropbox on your iPad.

*   **On your iPad,** you can share any file in your Dropbox by dragging a file into your Public folder, and you can sync files that you've marked as favorites in Dropbox.

In the following sections, we show you how to log in to Dropbox on your iPad, favorite a file in Dropbox, sync individual files in Dropbox, and share a file and a folder using Dropbox.

Syncing files in Dropbox works a little differently on an iPad than it does on a computer. On a computer, the files in your Dropbox sync automatically, but on an iPad, files sync on demand. You have to mark any file you want to sync on your iPad as a favorite before you can sync, so we present those tasks in that order.

Getting the software:

1. Register for a free Dropbox account at www.dropbox.com.

2. Download the software for your operating system (Mac, Windows, or Linux).

3. Download the free Dropbox for iPad app from the App Store.

Logging in to Dropbox:

1. Launch Dropbox by tapping its icon.

   You see the login screen (**Figure 2.4**).

Figure 2.4
The Dropbox login screen.

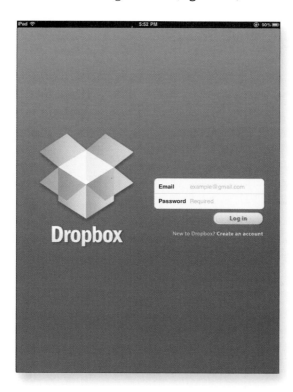

2. Enter the email address and password you used to register with Dropbox; then tap Log in.

    You see the Welcome to Dropbox! screen (**Figure 2.5**).

My Dropbox icon

Figure 2.5 Dropbox welcome screen.

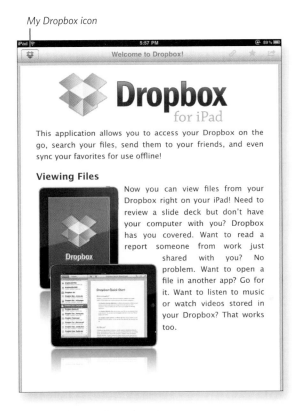

3. Tap the My Dropbox icon.

    You see the My Dropbox popover (**Figure 2.6** on the next page). (Your list of folders and files may look different.) Dropbox automatically creates the Photos and Public folders for you; these folders have special properties and purposes.

 You can create a new folder by tapping the plus sign in the bottom-left corner of any Dropbox file list, including the My Dropbox popover.

 My Dropbox is the heart of Dropbox on an iPad. Almost everything you do with the app starts with My Dropbox.

Figure 2.6
My Dropbox popover.

Favoriting a file in Dropbox:

1. Launch the Dropbox app on your iPad.

   You should see the My Dropbox popover (refer to Figure 2.6). If you don't see My Dropbox, tap the My Dropbox icon.

2. Tap a file in the list.

   The file opens in Dropbox's preview screen (**Figure 2.7**).

Favorite button

Link button   Action button

Figure 2.7 Dropbox
preview screen.

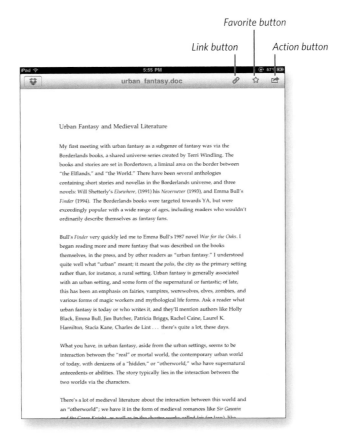

3. Tap the Favorite button at the right end of the screen's toolbar.

    The star turns dark to indicate that you've marked the file as
    a favorite. You also see a small star-in-blue-circle badge on the
    icons of any files you've favorited in Dropbox lists.

    **When you favorite a file, it's downloaded to your iPad so that you can
    read it even offline.**

Syncing on demand:

1. Tap the Home button in the top-left corner of the My Dropbox
    popover (refer to Figure 2.6 earlier in this project).

    The Home popover opens.

2. Tap Favorites.

You see a Favorites popover. Any files that need to be synced and updated to a later version on another device have a green-circle-and-white-arrow badge on their icons.

3. Tap a single file to update and sync it, or tap the Update All button in the bottom-right corner.

The icon badges change to a small green circle with a white check to reflect that the files have been updated (**Figure 2.8**).

Figure 2.8 Dropbox icon badge showing updated status for a synced file.

Sharing a file via Dropbox:

1. Open the file in Dropbox.

2. Tap the Link button in the top-right corner of the screen (refer to Figure 2.7).

The resulting popover displays two options: Email Link and Copy Link to Clipboard (**Figure 2.9**).

Figure 2.9 Popover showing linking options.

3. Tap Email Link.

You may briefly see a spinning-gear "busy" screen, followed by an email invitation containing the link (**Figure 2.10**).

Figure 2.10 Email invitation to share a Dropbox file.

4. Add an address to the email, and possibly a note; then tap Send.

   The recipient doesn't have to have a Dropbox account to access the linked file; he just clicks the link in your email and downloads the file.

Sharing a folder via Dropbox:

1. Open Safari on your iPad, and go to www.dropbox.com.

2. Log in to your Dropbox account.

   You see your home page (**Figure 2.11**).

Figure 2.11 Dropbox home page on the Web.

3. Tap the Sharing tab at the top of the page.

A page like **Figure 2.12** opens.

Figure 2.12
Sharing page.

4. Tap the Share a Folder button in the top center of the page.

You see a dialog like the one in **Figure 2.13**.

Figure 2.13
Sharing-options dialog.

5. Select the radio button titled I'd like to create and share a new folder, and type **Shared project files** in the adjacent field; then tap the blue Next button.

   You see a form like the one shown in **Figure 2.14**.

Figure 2.14
Web-sharing invitation.

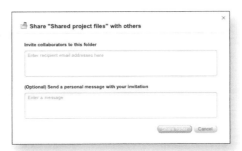

6. Enter email addresses in the top field and a short message in the bottom field; then tap the blue Share folder button.

 note **You can share a folder with someone who doesn't have Dropbox installed on her computer but who has a Dropbox account. She can access the folder via www.dropbox.com.**

 After a second or so, you see your new shared folder (**Figure 2.15**). If you look in My Dropbox on your iPad, you'll see the new folder there too. Shared folders have a badge on their icon like the one shown in the margin.

Figure 2.15 A new shared folder.

Your collaborators receive your email invitation with a link inviting them to join the shared folder. (It's a good idea to email them first to let them know to watch for the invitation from Dropbox.) After they do, you receive a confirmation email.

 You can place files or other folders in a shared folder and share the contents with anyone whom you invite. Your collaborators can also add and remove folders and files.

Get started with GoodReader

GoodReader is a reader designed for the iPad. It can read many kinds of files, and even share them, but it is most useful for reading and annotating PDF files. In this project, we show you how to transfer files to GoodReader, personalize your annotations, and annotate a PDF file.

 We can't possibly cover all the things you can do with GoodReader. To find out more, tap the question-mark icon in any screen in GoodReader, or visit the helpful manual at www.goodreader.net/gr-man.html.

Getting the app:

• Purchase (for $4.99) and download the GoodReader app from the App Store.

Transfer a file from a computer to GoodReader

Email isn't the only way to transfer files to your iPad. You can use iTunes to copy files to your computer from your iPad and from your iPad to your computer. When your iPad is connected to your computer via a USB port and the dock connector, the iTunes Apps tab contains a File Sharing section.

In the following task, we show how to transfer files from your computer to GoodReader, but the process is the same for any app that supports iTunes file transfer.

GoodReader uses the iPad's built in viewing engine (see the "Mail Attachments That the iPad Can Preview" sidebar earlier in this project) as well as its own to read the following file types: .pdf, .txt, .jpg, .jpeg, .gif, .tif, .tiff, .bmp, .bmpf, .png, .ico, .cur, and .xbm.

Transferring files to your iPad via iTunes:

1. Connect your iPad to your computer.

2. Launch iTunes, if it doesn't open automatically.

3. Select your iPad in the iTunes Source list.

4. In the main iTunes window, click the iPad's Apps tab.

5. Scroll down until you see the File Sharing pane (**Figure 2.16**).

Figure 2.16 iTunes File Sharing pane.

This section may look different if you have different apps installed on your iPad or if you use Windows instead of Mac OS X.

6. Select GoodReader in the Apps list on the left side of the pane.

   A GoodReader Documents list appears (**Figure 2.17** on the next page).

Figure 2.17
GoodReader
Documents list.

7. Click the Add button in the bottom-right corner of the pane.

   You see a familiar Open dialog for Windows or for Mac.

8. Navigate to and select the files you want to transfer to your iPad.

   For this task, select Word, PDF, and ePub files.

9. Click the Choose button.

   Your selected files appear in the GoodReader Documents list
   (**Figure 2.18**).

   When the file is in GoodReader for iPad, you can read and annotate
   it, as we show you in the following section.

Figure 2.18
The Documents list
with new files.

On a Mac, instead of completing steps 8 and 9, you can drag a file from a Finder window to the Pages Documents list.

 If you want to transfer a file from your iPad to your computer via iTunes, the process is almost exactly the same until step 7; to transfer a file from your iPad to your computer, click the Save button.

Download and read files from Dropbox in GoodReader

In the following tasks, we show you how to connect GoodReader with your Dropbox account and download files.

Adding a Dropbox server to GoodReader:

1. Launch GoodReader.

   You see the My Documents screen (**Figure 2.19**).

Figure 2.19
My Documents screen.

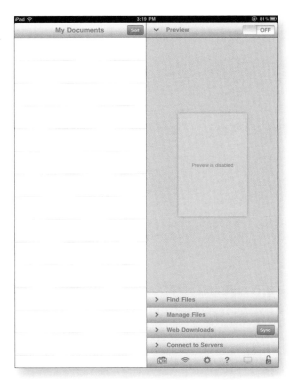

> tip   **The switch in the top-right corner toggles document previews. Tap the switch to turn it on if you want to see previews of documents and images.**

2. Below the Preview list, tap the Connect to Servers bar.

    You see the buttons shown in **Figure 2.20**.

Figure 2.20 Connect to Servers bar.

3. Tap the Add button.

    The Create New Connection popover opens (**Figure 2.21**), listing the servers GoodReader can connect to.

Figure 2.21 Create New Connection popover.

4. Tap Dropbox.

   A Dropbox login screen opens (**Figure 2.22**).

Figure 2.22 Dropbox login screen.

5. Enter a title in the Readable Title field.

   The name that you give this server account (such as iPad Projects DB) will identify it for you when it appears in the list of servers in the My Documents screen. You must enter something in this field.

6. (Optional) Enter your Dropbox login information in the User and Password fields.

   If you leave these fields empty, GoodReader will ask you for the information each time you access your Dropbox account from GoodReader.

7. Tap the blue Add button in the top-right corner.

   Your new Dropbox server is added to the Connect to Servers bar in the My Documents screen (**Figure 2.23**).

Figure 2.23 Connect to Servers bar showing the new server.

Downloading a file to GoodReader:

1. Open GoodReader.

2. Navigate to the My Documents screen, tapping the My Documents button if that screen isn't open.

3. Tap your Dropbox server in the Connect to Servers bar (refer to Figure 2.23).

   You see a popover similar to the one in **Figure 2.24**.

Figure 2.24 Dropbox server popover.

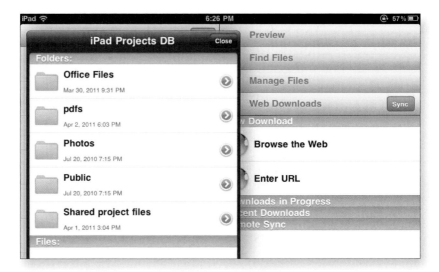

4. Select a file to view in GoodReader (**Figure 2.25**).

   For this task, select a PDF file, but the steps are the same for opening any type of file.

Figure 2.25 Selected PDF file.

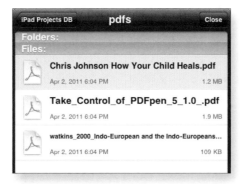

note If you've created folders in Dropbox, tap the blue > icon next to a folder's name to see its contents.

5. Tap the Download button in the bottom-right corner of the popover.

    A My Documents popover opens (**Figure 2.26**). The dialog in the figure shows previously downloaded files, which are dimmed and unavailable.

Figure 2.26
My Documents popover.

6. Tap the Download File Here button in the bottom-right corner of the My Documents popover.

    If you're very observant, or if the file is quite large, you may see a downloading progress bar. Then the downloaded PDF file is listed in the My Documents screen (**Figure 2.27**).

Figure 2.27
My Documents screen showing the newly downloaded file.

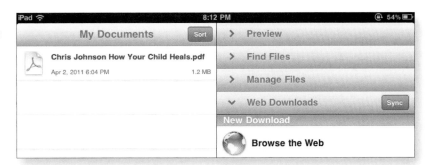

If you opened a folder in Dropbox, tap the Close button in the top-right corner of the folder's popover.

Reading a PDF in GoodReader:

1. Launch GoodReader, and tap a file in the My Documents screen.

    For this task, select a PDF file, but the procedure is the same for any type of file.

    You see a screen that's similar to **Figure 2.28**, showing the first page of the PDF file. The navigation bar at the bottom of the screen disappears fairly quickly to let you concentrate on reading.

Figure 2.28 First page of a PDF.

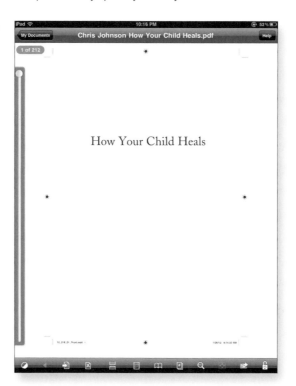

If you haven't used GoodReader much on your iPad, you may see pop-up tips or animated arrows and question marks. These elements are part of GoodReader's interactive help system, attempting to be helpful.

2. Tap the center of the screen to make the navigation bar reappear, along with the scroll bar on the left side of the screen (**Figure 2.29**).

Figure 2.29
GoodReader's scroll bar and navigation bar.

The buttons in the navigation bar (**Figure 2.30**) perform the following functions:

Figure 2.30
PDF navigation bar.

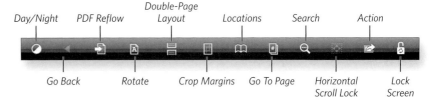

- **Day/Night** toggles the screen between black text on a white background (for reading by day) to white text on a black background (for reading at night).

- **Go Back** is similar to the Back button in a Web browser. Tapping this button takes you back one page in your GoodReader history.

- **PDF Reflow** extracts text from a PDF page so that you can read it comfortably, without left/right scrolling and in the font size of your choice. Tap the button again to return to the PDF file.

- **Rotate** rotates a file, which is useful for files that contain scanned images.

- **Double-Page Layout** lets you view two pages at a time.

- **Crop Margins** temporarily reduces margins to save screen space.

- **Locations** displays your own bookmarks, the table of contents, and your annotations for the current PDF (covered later in this project).

- **Go To Page** lets you enter a page number to find.

- **Search** lets you search for text within the document.

- **Horizontal Scroll Lock** toggles horizontal scroll lock. When the lock is on, you can move a page only vertically. This button appears with other kinds of files.

- **Action** performs different tasks based on the kind of file being viewed. It always includes options to email the file, to open it in another app on the iPad, and to delete it.

- **Screen Lock** locks screen rotation temporarily.

3. Read the file as you'd read any other onscreen file.

Annotate PDFs in GoodReader

Annotating PDFs—making notes that contain your name or initials—makes it easier for your colleagues who share files with you to keep track of who said what.

In this section, we show you how to personalize GoodReader so that your initials or name will be associated with the annotations you make in the next task.

Personalizing GoodReader's PDF settings:

1. Open GoodReader's My Documents screen.

2. Tap the gear icon at the bottom of the screen to display GoodReader's Settings popover (**Figure 2.31**).

Figure 2.31 Settings popover.

3. Tap Viewing PDF files.

   The PDF files popover opens (**Figure 2.32**).

Figure 2.32 PDF files popover.

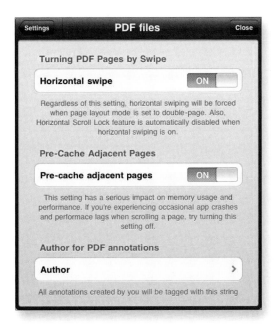

4. Tap the Author field.

5. Enter your name or initials in the pop-up Author dialog
   (**Figure 2.33**), and tap OK.

Figure 2.33
Author dialog.

Annotating a PDF file:

1. Open a PDF file in GoodReader.

2. Tap and hold anywhere on the PDF page where you want to add a note.

 When you tap and hold, GoodReader attempts to select the nearest word in preparation for an annotation. Use the drag handles to increase or decrease the selection.

The annotation bar appears (**Figure 2.34**).

Figure 2.34
Annotation bar.

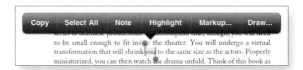

3. Tap Note.

   If you're making your first annotation or modification in a PDF, a dialog like the one shown in **Figure 2.35** appears. This dialog appears only the first time; it doesn't appear again.

Figure 2.35 You can annotate a copy or the original PDF file.

4. Tap Save to this file.

   The yellow window shown in **Figure 2.36** appears, ready for you to type a note.

transformation that will shrink you to the same size as the actors. Properly
miniaturized, you can then watch the drama unfold. Think of this book as
Close
LLS
Save

Figure 2.36 A note annotation.

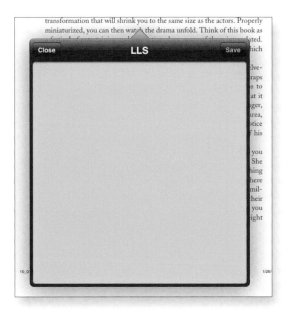

5. Type something in the window and then tap the Save button.

   A yellow note marker appears on the PDF page (**Figure 2.37**).

This book will make you a front-row spectator in the audience for a series of dramatic productions. To accomplish that, though, you will need to be small enough to fit inside the theater. You will undergo a virtual transformation that will shrink you to the same size as the actors. Properly miniaturized, you can then watch the drama unfold. Think of this book as a festival of entertaining and instructive plays, many of them interrelated. To take it all in, you will make a succession of expeditions, each of which reveals some aspect of how healing works.

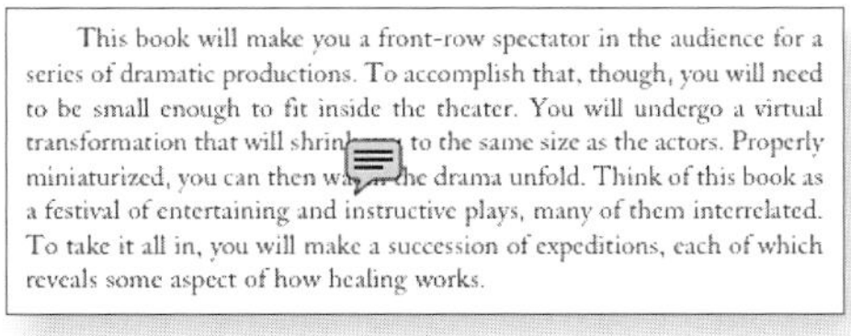

Figure 2.37 Note marker.

tip

Tap the marker to see your note, tap and hold the marker to see a menu of editing options, or tap and hold and drag the note (after a delay) to move it to a new location.

6. Tap and hold somewhere else on the page to display the annotation bar, and use the drag handles to select several words of text.

7. Tap Highlight in the annotation bar (refer to Figure 2.34).

    The passage of text you selected is highlighted in the PDF file
    (**Figure 2.38**).

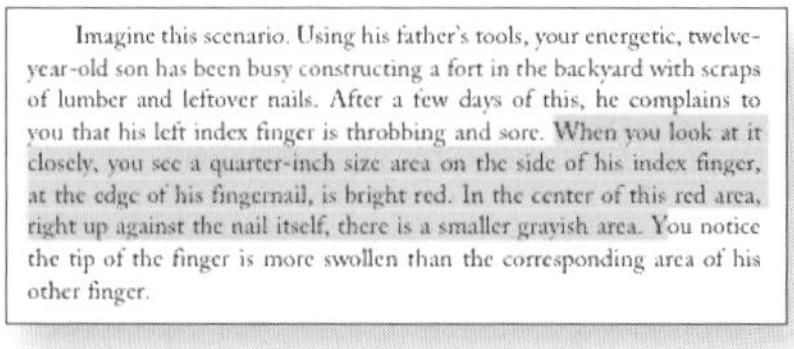

Figure 2.38
Highlighting in
GoodReader.

Imagine this scenario. Using his father's tools, your energetic, twelve-year-old son has been busy constructing a fort in the backyard with scraps of lumber and leftover nails. After a few days of this, he complains to you that his left index finger is throbbing and sore. When you look at it closely, you see a quarter-inch size area on the side of his index finger, at the edge of his fingernail, is bright red. In the center of this red area, right up against the nail itself, there is a smaller grayish area. You notice the tip of the finger is more swollen than the corresponding area of his other finger.

tip   If you tap the highlighted area, you can modify the highlight by adding
a note, changing the color, or deleting it.

8. Tap Markup or Draw in the annotation bar.

    A new button bar appears.

9. Experiment with the options in the new button bar to annotate the
    PDF further.

tip   All of GoodReader's annotation tools work with either a quick tap or a
tap and hold. If one technique doesn't do what you expect, try the other.

Use Instapaper to read on the go

Instapaper allows you to save articles or blog posts in a Web browser to
read later, even on another computer, a smartphone, or an iPad. After you
link your Instapaper account to one of the supported social-networking
services, you also have an option to share stories through Facebook,
Twitter, Tumblr, Pinboard, Evernote, and many other apps and services.

In this section, we show you how to open your free Instapaper account
and get the Instapaper app.

note   It's quite possible to use Instapaper only on your iPad, but if you
browse the Web on more than one device, it's convenient to have
access to your saved content everywhere.

Getting started with Instapaper:

1. On your computer, go to www.instapaper.com, and click the Create Account link.

2. Follow the onscreen instructions to create your account.

You can create a free account in the Instapaper app on your iPad, but creating an account on a computer where you may be marking things to read later will save you a step.

3. On your iPad, purchase and download the Instapaper app from the App Store.

4. Launch the Instapaper app on your iPad.

   You see the login screen (**Figure 2.39**).

Figure 2.39 Instapaper login screen.

5. Enter your email address and Instapaper password; then tap Done on your iPad's onscreen keyboard.

   The Read Later screen opens (**Figure 2.40**). This screen is where you'll find content that you've saved to read later.

Figure 2.40 Read Later screen.

Install the Read it Later bookmarklet

To use Instapaper to mark Web content for later reading on both your computer and iPad, you need to install the Instapaper bookmarklet on your computer's Web browser and in Safari on your iPad, as we show you how to do in this section.

Installing the Read it Later bookmarklet on your iPad is laborious because of the way Safari works on the iPad. If you use Safari on your computer, it's much easier to install the Read it Later bookmarklet there and sync with your iPad. We show you both methods in the following tasks.

Installing the bookmarklet in any Web browser on your computer:

1. On your computer, launch your preferred Web browser.

2. Go to www.instapaper.com/extras.

3. Follow the instructions on the page to install the bookmarklet in your Web browser.

The Read it Later bookmarklet works beautifully in the Mac OS X and Windows versions of Mozilla Firefox and Google Chrome, as well as in Safari (see the next task). Just drag the bookmarklet to your toolbar or bookmark bar.

Installing the bookmarklet in Safari on your computer:

1. Launch Safari on your computer.

2. Go to www.instapaper.com/extras.

3. Follow the instructions on the page to install the bookmarklet in Safari.

4. Sync your iPad and your computer, following the instructions in the **Information Syncing Project** in Chapter 1 of this book.

    Your bookmarklet is magically transported to Safari on your iPad, along with your other Safari bookmarks.

> **tip**
>
> **If the bookmarks bar isn't visible in Safari on your iPad, open the Settings app, tap Safari, and select Always Show Bookmarks Bar.**

Installing the bookmarklet in Safari on your iPad:

1. Launch and log in to Instapaper on your iPad.

2. Tap the Settings button at the top of the Read Later screen (refer to Figure 2.40 earlier in this project).

   You see the Settings popover (**Figure 2.41**).

Figure 2.41 Instapaper Settings popover.

3. Tap Install "Read Later" in Safari.

4. Follow the instructions on your iPad's screen.

Save and read content in Instapaper

Now that you have Instapaper and the Read it Later bookmarklet installed, you can save Web pages for reading later in Instapaper.

Saving and reading Web content:

1. Find a page on the Web that you want to read later.

2. Select the Read it Later bookmarklet in your browser's toolbar.

   A graphic flashes in the top-left corner of the browser page, saying first *Instapaper Saving* and then *Instapaper Saved!*

3. Launch and log in to the Instapaper app on your iPad.

   The Read Later screen lists your saved content (**Figure 2.42**) and offers several options:

   • The Folders button lets you see a list of folders, as well as create new folders.

   • The Edit button lets you select articles to be deleted permanently.

   • The Friends and Editors buttons display article lists saved by your friends and by specially selected Instapaper editors.

   • The Web button lets you browse for more content directly in Instapaper.

Figure 2.42 Read Later screen with content.

4. Tap an article in the list to read it.

   You see the article reformatted for the screen (**Figure 2.43**).

Figure 2.43 An article screen in Instapaper.

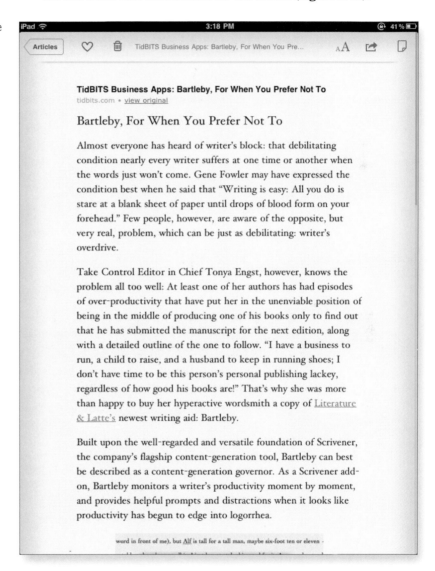

 You can also share Web content that you've saved in Instapaper with colleagues via email or by using several apps listed at www.instapaper.com/extras.

iPad Chef Project

Difficulty level: Easy

Software needed: Epicurious Recipes & Shopping List 3.0 app (free), BigOven app (free), Apple's Pages for iPad ($9.99)

iPad model: Any

Additional hardware: Kitchen and camera (optional)

This project is about finding recipes with the Epicurious and BigOven apps, favoriting the recipes you want to try, emailing recipes that you want to share, and creating your own recipe scrapbook in Pages for iPad.

Find recipes with Epicurious

Long before the iPad, there were cookbooks; glossy cooking and food magazines, many with equally glossy Web sites; and large community sites for cooks and lovers of food of all sorts. There still are. With so many resources available, searching for just the right recipe can be confusing.

Fortunately, iPad apps are available to save you time and effort. Epicurious.com, the Web home of *Epicurious* magazine, recently released a version of its iPhone app for the iPad. This free app (available at the App Store) makes it easy to browse or search thousands of recipes provided by *Gourmet* and *Bon Appetit* magazines, professional chefs, popular cookbooks, and famous restaurants. Here's how.

Using Epicurious to browse recipes:

1. Tap the Epicurious icon on your iPad to launch the app.

   The Epicurious splash screen appears very briefly, followed by the home screen, with its Control Panel popover showing recipes in the Featured category (**Figure 2.44**).

   The categories change based on season, so your Control Panel will be different from the figure. It may also display an advertisement for additional pay-for features.

Figure 2.44 Epicurious home screen.

2. Tap one of the categories to browse recipes by type.

    You see a screen that looks very much like a page in a printed cook-book, with navigational tabs along the right side (**Figure 2.45** on the next page).

3. Tap a recipe to see that recipe in its own screen, with the Ingredients popover open (**Figure 2.46** on the next page).

Figure 2.45 Category screen.

Figure 2.46 Recipe screen with Ingredients popover.

4. Tap the recipe to make the Ingredients window disappear and see information about preparing the dish (**Figure 2.47**).

Figure 2.47
Recipe screen.

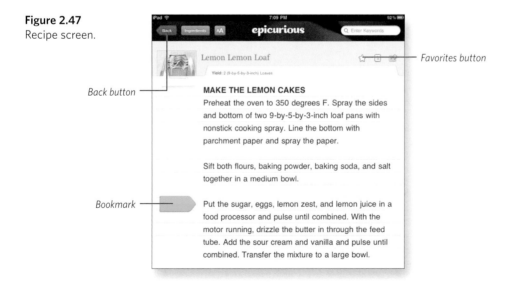

Navigating Epicurious

Thousands of recipes are available via Epicurious, and more are added all the time. Navigating this sea of recipes can be tricky, so here are a few hints:

- Tap a tab on the right side of a category screen to see the relevant view: Rating (recipe ratings by other cooks), Photo (recipes with images), A-Z (recipes in the category listed alphabetically), or Newest (most recently added recipes in the category).

- The colored navigation tabs at the bottom of recipe screens provide more information. Reviews displays comments by other cooks who have tried the recipe; About describes the source of the recipe. Some recipes offer other tabs that provide additional information, such as nutrition data.

- The gray navigation triangles in the bottom-right corner of every page go to the preceding and next recipe in the current category. The text between them identifies the recipe's location in its category—such as *5 of 86* for the 5th recipe of the 86 in that category.

- Each recipe screen has an orange bookmark (refer to Figure 2.47). You can slide this bookmark up or down to mark your spot in the recipe, which makes it easy to keep track while you work in the kitchen.

- Tapping the house icon on category screens always takes you to the home screen.

5. For purposes of this project, tap the red Back button in the top-left corner of the recipe screen to return to the preceding category screen.

A display bug in version 3.0 of Epicurious may prevent the Back button from appearing. If you're viewing a single-recipe screen and don't see this button, rotate your iPad to change its orientation. The button will appear.

Searching for recipes in Epicurious:

1. If a category screen isn't already open on your iPad, tap the Back button to reach a category screen.

2. Tap the gray Control Panel button in the top-left corner of the screen.

   The Control Panel popover appears (refer to Figure 2.44 earlier in this project). Notice the row of buttons along the top (**Figure 2.48**).

Figure 2.48 Control Panel buttons.

3. Tap the Search button at the top of the control panel to perform advanced searches.

   You can search for a specific type of food or drink, a meal or course, the main ingredient in a recipe, or a cuisine. You can even search by dietary restriction or special occasion.

 You can also search via the Search field in the top-right corner of each recipe screen, but that field limits you to a keyword search.

   When you find a recipe you like by browsing or searching, you can favorite the recipe, much as you might bookmark a Web site, so that you can find it easily later. In the next task, we show you how.

Favoriting Epicurious recipes:

1. Tap the Epicurious icon to open the app, if it isn't already open.

2. Locate a recipe that you want to be able to find later (see the preceding two tasks).

   When you're looking at that recipe's page, you'll find a white star to the right of the recipe title (refer to Figure 2.47).

3. Tap the star to favorite the recipe.

   The star turns blue to show that the recipe has been added to your favorites list.

 If you want to remove a recipe from your favorites list, tap its blue star. The recipe is deleted from the list, and its star reverts to white.

Displaying your Epicurious favorites:

1. Launch Epicurious, if it isn't already open.

2. If the control panel doesn't appear on the home page, tap the gray Control Panel button in the top-left corner.

3. Tap the Favorites button at the top of the control panel.

   The My Favorites screen opens (**Figure 2.49**). (Yours will be different from ours, of course.)

Figure 2.49
My Favorites screen.

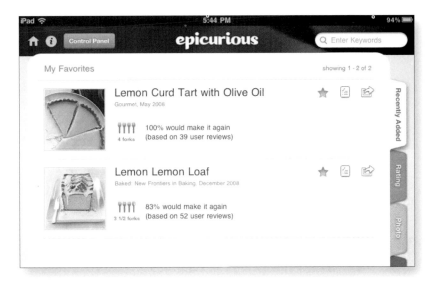

Each recipe in the list has three icons to the right of its title, as shown in **Figure 2.50**. All these icons work the same way wherever they occur in Epicurious.

Shopping List button

Favorites button   Action button

Figure 2.50
My Favorites screen recipe icons.

The Action button, for example, displays a popover when you tap it (**Figure 2.51**). The More option in this popover makes it easy for you to share recipes via email, Twitter, Facebook, and many other services, including Instapaper (discussed in the **Go to Meeting Project** earlier in this chapter).

Figure 2.51 Action-button popover.

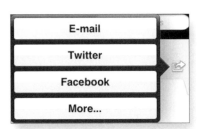

Viewing and emailing a recipe's shopping list in Epicurious:

1. Display your My Favorites screen (see the preceding task).

2. Tap the Shopping List button to the right of a recipe's name (refer to Figure 2.50) to generate a shopping list for that recipe.

 If you tap the Shopping List button for other recipes in your My Favorites screens, those recipes' shopping lists are combined with the first.

3. Display the shopping list by tapping the Control Panel button in the top-left corner to open the Control Panel popover and then tapping My Shopping List at the bottom of that screen.

   You see a nicely laid-out My Combined Shopping List screen (**Figure 2.52**).

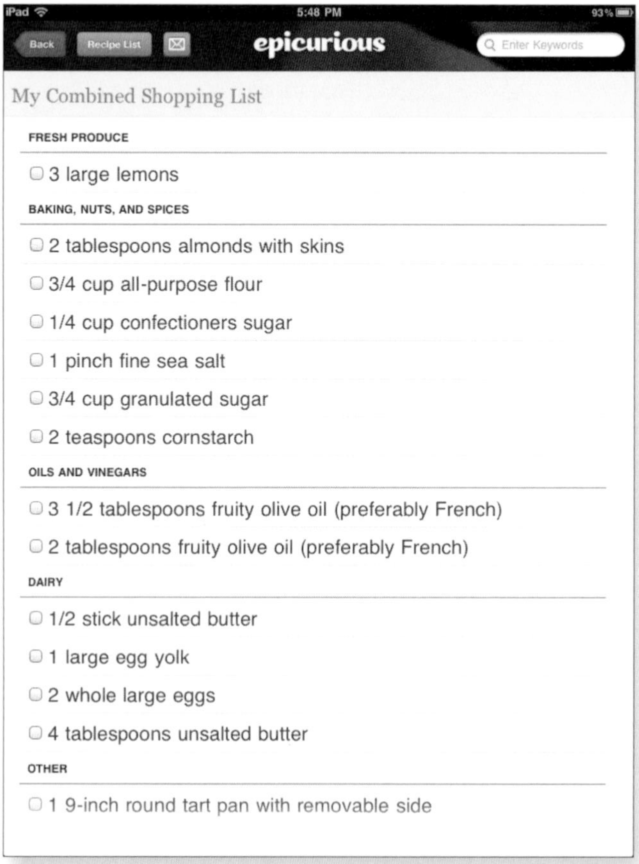

Figure 2.52
My Combined Shopping List screen.

iPad 📶   5:48 PM   93% 🔋

[Back] [Recipe List] [✉]   **epicurious**   [🔍 Enter Keywords]

My Combined Shopping List

FRESH PRODUCE
- ☐ 3 large lemons

BAKING, NUTS, AND SPICES
- ☐ 2 tablespoons almonds with skins
- ☐ 3/4 cup all-purpose flour
- ☐ 1/4 cup confectioners sugar
- ☐ 1 pinch fine sea salt
- ☐ 3/4 cup granulated sugar
- ☐ 2 teaspoons cornstarch

OILS AND VINEGARS
- ☐ 3 1/2 tablespoons fruity olive oil (preferably French)
- ☐ 2 tablespoons fruity olive oil (preferably French)

DAIRY
- ☐ 1/2 stick unsalted butter
- ☐ 1 large egg yolk
- ☐ 2 whole large eggs
- ☐ 4 tablespoons unsalted butter

OTHER
- ☐ 1 9-inch round tart pan with removable side

4. To email yourself a copy of a recipe, tap the red Back button in the top-left corner of the My Combined Shopping List screen to return to your My Favorites screen; then tap the Action button to the right of the recipe you want to send.

    You see the Action-button popover (refer to Figure 2.51).

5. Tap E-mail.

    Epicurious creates a blank email ready for you to add addresses, with the Subject line listing the recipe's title and the body containing the recipe (**Figure 2.53**).

Figure 2.53
Epicurious recipe in a ready-to-address email.

> Cancel   **Recipe for Lemon Lemon Loaf from...**   Send
>
> To:
>
> Cc/Bcc, From: ipadprojects@gmail.com
>
> Subject: Recipe for Lemon Lemon Loaf from Epicurious.com
>
> This **Epicurious.com** recipe: Lemon Lemon Loaf has been sent to you by a friend.
>
> You can view the complete recipe online at:
> http://www.epicurious.com/recipes/food/views/Lemon-Lemon-Loaf-350989?mbid=ipapp

6. Add the recipient's email address and a brief message.

    For this task, address the email to yourself.

7. Tap the Send button.

    In a minute or two, if you check your email, you should see a nicely formatted recipe in your inbox.

Get the BigOven app and create an account

You need to download the free BigOven app from the App Store. You also need a free BigOven account if you want to sync favorite recipes with the Web site and your iPad (or smartphone).

note **The $15.99 paid BigOven app allows you to create grocery shopping lists that sync across devices, email grocery lists, and look up terms in a glossary. It's also ad-free.**

In the following tasks, you use the free version. though the steps work for both versions.

Getting started with BigOven:

1. Get the BigOven app from the App Store.

2. Go to www.bigoven.com.

3. Click the Join Us! button to create a free account.

Entering your BigOven account info in the app:

1. Tap the Settings icon on your iPad to open the Settings screen.

2. Tap BigOven in the Apps section on the left side of the screen.

   The app's account settings appear on the right side (**Figure 2.54**).

Figure 2.54 BigOven account settings.

3. Enter your account email address and password in the BigOven Account section.

4. Press the iPad's Home button to exit Settings.

Find recipes with BigOven

BigOven began as a Web site for people who love to cook but who face the never-ending question "What do I make for dinner tonight?" on a regular basis. The Web site and apps are designed to help people plan meals and exchange recipes.

Searching for recipes in BigOven:

1. Tap the BigOven icon to launch the app.

2. Tap the BigOven button in the top-left corner of the splash screen.

   You see the BigOven navigation popover (**Figure 2.55**), which displays categories you can search.

Figure 2.55 BigOven navigation popover.

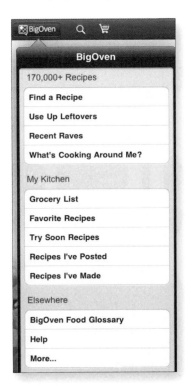

3. Tap Find a Recipe.

A search form opens (**Figure 2.56**).

Figure 2.56
Search form.

You can perform a variety of searches, including those restricted to the title of a recipe or keywords. The basic functions of all search types are the same, however, so we'll go through one search step by step and leave the other types for you to explore on your own.

4. Tap the Leftovers button at the top of the search form.

You see a search window similar to the one shown in **Figure 2.57**.

5. Select up to three leftover ingredients in the spin wheels (**Figure 2.58**), and tap the large red Search BigOven button.

A list of search results appears (**Figure 2.59**).

Figure 2.57 Leftovers search form.

Figure 2.58 Leftovers search form showing search terms.

Figure 2.59 Leftovers recipe search results.

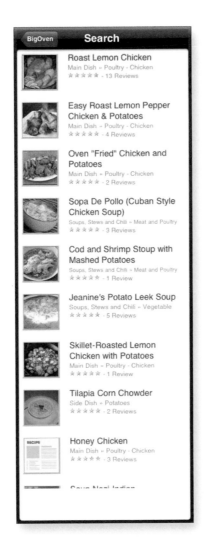

6. Tap a recipe in the list of search results.

   The app displays the recipe in easy-to-read form (**Figure 2.60** on the next page).

 Tap the Prepare button to view the recipe without ads or extraneous data so you can follow the instructions easily when you're preparing the dish.

Prepare button   Action button

Figure 2.60
Recipe screen.

7. If you want to return to the search results from a recipe screen, tap the BigOven button in the top-left corner.

Mark and find favorite recipes in BigOven

When you've found a recipe you like, it's useful to mark it as a favorite so that you can find it again easily, as we show you in the following tasks.

Marking favorite recipes in BigOven:

1. Tap BigOven's icon to open the app, if it isn't already open.

2. Find a recipe you like (see the preceding task).

3. Tap the Action button at the far-right end of the toolbar (refer to Figure 2.60).

   You see the options shown in **Figure 2.61**.

Figure 2.61
Action-button popover options.

Add to Favorites

Add to Try Soon

Email it

Share on Twitter

Share on Facebook

Review it

View Ingredients as Metric

4. Tap Add to Favorites.

BigOven adds the recipe to your favorites list.

 After you favorite a recipe, Add to Favorites is replaced by Remove from Favorites in the Action-button popover. Tap it to remove the recipe.

Viewing favorite recipes in BigOven:

1. Tap the BigOven button in the top-left corner of the screen.

You see the navigation popover (refer to Figure 2.55 earlier in this project).

2. In the My Kitchen section, tap Favorite Recipes to see your favorites (**Figure 2.62**).

Figure 2.62
Favorites list.

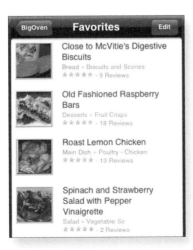

Share BigOven recipes

After you find and favorite recipes, you can email them to yourself or to a friend, as you see in the next task.

Emailing a recipe from BigOven:

1. Launch BigOven, if it isn't already running.

2. Find a recipe by searching for it (see "Searching for recipes in BigOven" earlier in this project), or tap a recipe in your favorites list (see the preceding task).

3. Tap the Action button at the far-right end of the toolbar.

   You see a list of options in a popover (refer to Figure 2.61).

4. Tap Email it.

   A formatted email message opens ,with your default email address displayed in the From field (**Figure 2.63**).

Figure 2.63 Recipe ready to email.

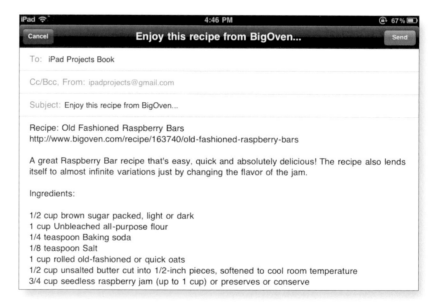

5. Enter the recipient's address, add a short message, and tap Send to send the email.

Create a recipe scrapbook in Pages

Now that you know how to find, favorite, and email recipes, the next step is creating a personal recipe collection on your iPad that you can add to at will. In the following tasks, you use Pages for iPad to create a recipe scrapbook.

Creating a recipe scrapbook is a great way not only to preserve your own recipes, but also to keep recipes that you've collected from the Internet or from friends who emailed their recipes to you. You can create an attractive recipe scrapbook quite easily in Pages for iPad. The process involves four steps:

1. Get the recipe text into Pages.

2. Prepare the dish (which we'll let you do on your own).

3. Take a picture of the finished dish.

4. Import and position the image in the Pages recipe.

You can enter a recipe directly in Pages or email it to yourself as a Microsoft Word file, a rich-text (.rtf) file, or a Pages file attachment and then import the file into Pages by using Mail's Open in option. For step-by-step instructions, see the **Go to Meeting Project** earlier in this chapter.

In the following tasks, we show you how to start your recipe scrapbook by importing an emailed recipe into Pages for iPad and then formatting it, adding artwork. You'll be working with the recipe for Old Fashioned Raspberry Bars from BigOven, which you can find in the BigOven app by searching for it by title (see "Searching for recipes in BigOven" earlier in this project).

Importing an emailed recipe into Pages:

1. Open a recipe that you received by email (see "Emailing a recipe from BigOven" earlier in this project).

    The recipe will have basic formatting even in email form (**Figure 2.64** on the next page).

Figure 2.64 Recipe emailed from BigOven.

2. Tap and hold anywhere in the body of the email except on a hyperlink.

You see Select and Select All buttons (**Figure 2.65**).

Figure 2.65 Selection buttons.

3. Tap Select All to select the entire body of the email—in this case, the recipe.

4. Tap the Copy button that appears.

The button briefly flashes blue to indicate that the selected text has been copied to your iPad's internal clipboard, ready to paste.

At this point, you could paste the selected text into the Notes app on your iPad, Trunk Notes, or one of the many simple note apps available for iPad. For this project, however, you use Pages because you want to include images.

5. Launch Pages on your iPad.

6. If you don't see the My Documents screen when Pages opens, tap the My Documents button in the top-left corner.

7. Tap the New Document button in the top-left corner of the My Documents screen.

   The Choose a Template screen opens (**Figure 2.66**).

Figure 2.66 Choose a Template screen.

8. Tap Blank.

   A blank document opens.

The document is automatically named Blank. You can change that title if you want in the My Documents screen (tap the word *Blank* below the file's icon and then type a new name), but for convenience, we'll refer to this document as Blank.

9. Tap and hold in the body of the document until you see Paste and Copy Style buttons (**Figure 2.67**).

Figure 2.67 Paste and Copy Style buttons.

10. Tap Paste.

The text you copied from the email in step 4 appears in the Pages document (**Figure 2.68**).

Figure 2.68
Text pasted from the iPad clipboard.

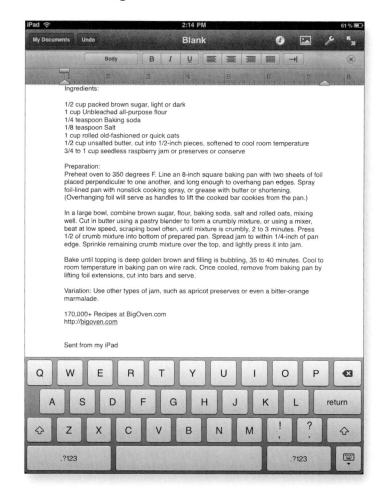

You'll use this Blank document as a staging document while you build the recipe scrapbook in the following task.

Creating a recipe file for your scrapbook:

1. Tap the Pages icon to open the app.

2. If Pages opens to a file instead of the My Documents window, tap the My Document button in the opening screen.

3. Tap the New Document button in the top-left corner of the My Documents screen.

4. Scroll down to tap the Recipe template.

   A document based on that template opens in Pages (**Figure 2.69**).

Figure 2.69
Recipe template.

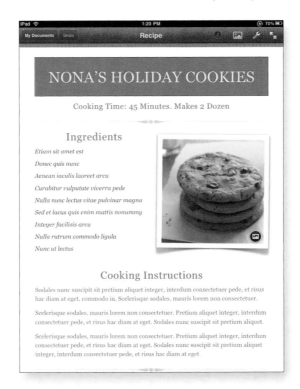

Pages names the new file Recipe by default, and you can change that name, but we'll refer to the document as Recipe in this project.

5. To change the title text from *Nona's Holiday Cookies,* rapidly triple-tap that text to select the entire line.

   A selection rectangle appears around the title.

6. Type new title text.

7. If you want to, tap and hold the text below the title to select and edit the cooking time and quantity of your recipe.

Copying recipe ingredients to the scrapbook:

1. Tap the My Documents button in the top-left corner of the recipe screen.

2. In the My Documents screen, tap to open the Blank document where you pasted the recipe (see "Importing an emailed recipe into Pages" earlier in this project).

3. Tap and hold to the left of where the ingredients list begins.

   Selection buttons appear (**Figure 2.70**).

Figure 2.70 Displaying selection buttons.

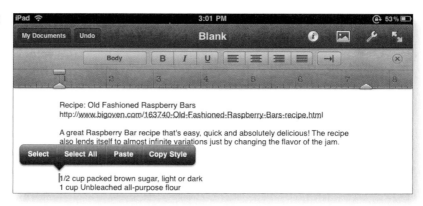

4. Tap Select, and drag the selection rectangle around the entire list of ingredients (**Figure 2.71**).

Figure 2.71 Selecting the ingredients list.

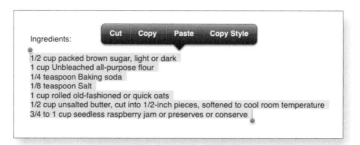

As soon as you lift your finger off the screen, the Copy button appears.

5. Tap Copy to copy the selected text to your iPad's clipboard.

6. Tap the My Documents button to open the My Documents screen.

7. Tap the Recipe document (see the preceding task) to open it.

8. Tap and hold to the left of the italic placeholder text that begins *Etiam sit amet est* to display selection buttons.

9. Tap Select.

    Pages selects the entire block of placeholder text and displays the Paste button (**Figure 2.72**).

Figure 2.72 Selecting placeholder text.

10. Tap Paste.

    The template's placeholder text is replaced by the ingredients for your recipe.

 If you want your ingredients list to be in italics, select the ingredients and then tap the *I* button on the Pages toolbar.

11. Repeat steps 1–10, copying the procedure or preparation section of your recipe from the Blank staging document and pasting it in the Cooking Instructions section of the Recipe document (**Figure 2.73** on the next page).

    Now all you need to do is replace the image from the template with the image for your recipe.

Figure 2.73
The Recipe document with all the template text replaced by a new recipe.

Customizing Recipes in Pages

You can extensively customize the documents that you make from Pages templates. Here are some ways you may want to customize your recipes:

- To change the font or color of text, select the text; tap the *I* button on the Pages toolbar; and then tap Style > Text in the popover that appears. You can set the size of text, the color, and the font.

- To change the background color of the title in a recipe file, tap the colored background area to select it; tap the *I* button on the Pages toolbar; tap Style in the form that appears; and choose a new background color.

- It's a good idea to include a note about where a recipe originated or who created it. You can simply copy the URL from the email and paste it into the recipe, or you can type a short note about your source.

Importing an image into Pages:

1. Launch Safari on your iPad.

2. Go to a Web site that has suitable images.

   For this task, go to the Old Fashioned Raspberry Bars page at www.bigoven.com/recipe/163740/old-fashioned-raspberry-bars.

3. Tap and hold the image you want to use.

   Open, Open in New Page, Save Image, and Copy buttons pop up (**Figure 2.74**).

Figure 2.74 Copying an image from a Web site.

4. Tap Save Image.

   The image is downloaded to your iPad's Photos app.

 Downloaded images are saved in the Saved Photos album on an original iPad and in the Photos app's Camera Roll album on an iPad 2.

Inserting an image into the scrapbook:

1. In Pages, open the Recipe document you created in "Creating a recipe file for your scrapbook" earlier in this project.

   If the document isn't currently open in Pages, tap the My Documents button; then tap the Recipe document's icon in the My Documents screen.

2. Tap the Image icon in the bottom-right corner of the placeholder image.

   The Photo Albums popover opens (**Figure 2.75**), listing the albums in your Photos app.

3. Tap Saved Photos or Camera Roll, depending on which iPad model you're using.

   You see the images that you've saved to your iPad, including the one you saved from a Web site in the preceding task (**Figure 2.76**).

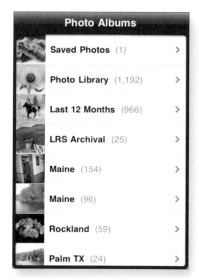

Figure 2.75 List of albums in Photos.

Figure 2.76 Saved Photos album showing the newly saved image.

4. Tap the image you saved from the Web site.

   Your image replaces the placeholder image in the template (**Figure 2.77**).

Figure 2.77
The template image replaced by the correct image.

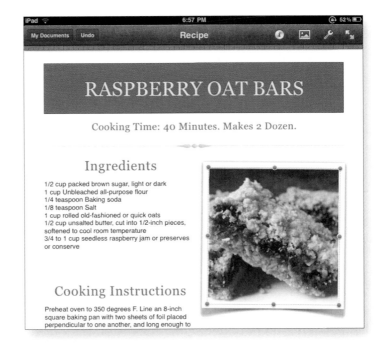

5. Adjust the size of the image, if you want, by tapping it and then dragging the selection rectangle.

6. Drag the image to a different place on the page, if you want.

Using an iPad in the Kitchen

Using an iPad in the kitchen can be truly labor-saving, but it can also be very risky. Electronic devices really aren't designed to spend time around bubbling liquids, for example. Here are a few tips to make cooking with an iPad easier and safer:

- **Stand it up.** Think about getting a stand for your iPad. An awful lot of people have found that a cookbook stand works perfectly for an iPad, though you may want to position it in a place that's somewhat sheltered.

- **Bag it up.** A gallon-size plastic food-storage bag (the kind with a zipper closure) makes a great protective cover for an iPad. Slip the iPad inside a clean dry bag, and seal it. The iPad will be a little less vulnerable to spills and splashes, and you can still use the touchscreen through the bag.

- **Keep it awake.** Consider changing the Auto-Lock setting (tap Settings > General) to keep your iPad from going to sleep and locking the screen at a crucial moment.

Flash Card Project

Difficulty level: Intermediate

Software needed: Keynote for iPad ($10)

iPad model: Any

Additional hardware: Optional AirPrint-compatible printer

Remember flash cards? Those old-school handheld teaching devices? Well, in this project, you're going to make some.

But put down the posterboard, the scissors, the glue stick, and the colored markers, because you won't be needing them. Instead, you'll make your flash cards on the iPad, using one for-pay app and your iPad's Safari Web browser.

The object of this particular project is to create a set of flash cards to teach words and phrases in another language, but the project really is open-ended. You can use the techniques you develop here to create flash cards on a variety of subjects.

Get your app in gear

Let's start by getting the app you need: Apple's Keynote for the iPad. Its icon is shown in **Figure 2.78**.

Figure 2.78
The Keynote app's icon.

Keynote for the iPad is a scaled-down version of the Keynote application that Apple sells in the Mac App Store. In its Macintosh incarnation, Keynote is a powerful alternative to the widely used Microsoft PowerPoint presentation application. Although the iPad incarnation of the software is somewhat less powerful (and less expensive), you can still make surprisingly sophisticated presentations with it.

In this project, you use Keynote to create a small deck of simple flash cards—a task well within its capabilities.

Acquiring Keynote:

- Purchase Keynote from the App Store, either directly on your iPad or via iTunes on your computer.

  Just in case you have trouble finding it (although you probably won't), you can open the following URL in a Web browser on your computer, which opens iTunes and takes you right to the app:

  http://itunes.apple.com/us/app/keynote/id361285480?mt=8

  As soon as you have this app installed on your iPad, you're ready to begin.

> **tip**
>
> **This project requires you to move back and forth between Keynote and Safari several times. To make all this navigation easier, you can use the Recent apps list. Double-click the Home button to reveal a panel that shows the currently running apps at the bottom of the screen; then tap the icon for the app you want to open.**

Translate some words and phrases

The flash-card deck you build can be as thick as you like (or as the storage of your iPad can accommodate). We're going to limit ourselves to three common and useful phrases here, but if you feel ambitious, feel free to add as many as you like. The language we'll use is Italian.

Here are the phrases:

- Hello. My name is _____.

- Where is the restroom?

- Excuse me. Would you take a picture of us?

To perform the translation, we'll use Google Translate, which we'll access with the Safari Web browser. This translation engine can translate dozens of languages, and even though it's not perfect, it's more than adequate for our purposes.

Translating with Google Translate:

1. Open Safari.

2.   Enter **http://translate.google.com** in the location bar and then tap Go on the onscreen keyboard.

    The appearance of this page can vary, because Google always likes to tinker with things. **Figure 2.79** shows the classic version of the page at this writing.

Figure 2.79
The Google Translate page in mobile Safari.

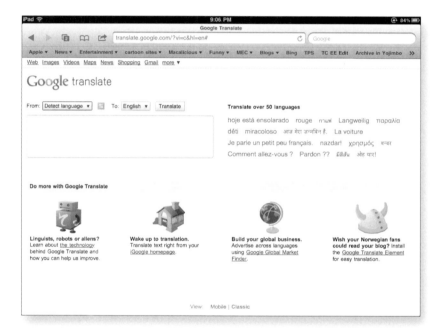

> **note**
>
> **Google may show you the mobile version of the page. The iPad is a mobile device, after all, and Google may detect that fact. The classic version of the page works fine on the large iPad screen, however, and it's easy to switch from one version to the other.**

3. If the Google Translate page shown is the mobile version, tap Classic at the bottom of the page.

4. Tap the To button above the text-entry field (**Figure 2.80**), and choose English from the drop-down list of languages; then tap the From button, and choose Italian from the drop-down list.

Figure 2.80 Use the From and To buttons to choose languages.

5. In the text-entry field, type a phrase to translate—in this case, **Hello. My name is _____.**

   As you type, Google displays the translated text, as shown in **Figure 2.81**.

Figure 2.81 Google translates your words as you type them.

6. Tap Return and then type the second phrase in our list of phrases: **Where is the restroom?**

   The translation of the second phrase appears below the translation of the first one.

7. Once again, tap Return and then type the third phrase in our list: **Excuse me. Would you take a picture of us?**

   Now all three translated phrases appear on the page (**Figure 2.82**).

Figure 2.82 All three translations are on the same page.

Collect some illustrations

All you really need for your flash cards in this project are Italian phrases and their translations, but flash cards are far more fun and attractive if you can spice them up with some illustrations. In this section, you use Safari to find and collect appropriate illustrations via Google's image search.

If you've completed the preceding steps, Safari is still open on your iPad. Fortunately, you don't have to discard the Google Translate page to search for images, because Safari allows you to have more than one page open at a time. You can move among the open Safari pages by tapping the Pages button in Safari's toolbar.

> **note** If more than one page is open in Safari, the Pages button displays a number showing how many pages you currently have open. You can have as many as nine pages open at the same time, if you want.

Gathering images with Google Images:

1. In Safari's toolbar, tap the Pages button.

   A black screen appears, containing small versions of the pages that are currently open in Safari (**Figure 2.83**).

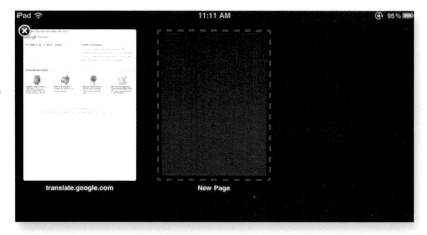

Figure 2.83 You can see which pages are open in Safari and tap one to work with, or you can tap New Page to open a different one.

2. In Safari, go to www.google.com/images.

3. On the Google Images page, type **il bagno** in the search field and then tap Search Images.

   Google displays a page of image results (**Figure 2.84**).

   In case you haven't guessed, *il bagno* is Italian for *bathroom,* and in fact, most of the images shown are of Italian bathrooms. You could have searched for *bathroom,* of course, but why not be authentic?

Figure 2.84 Google claims to have millions of Italian bathroom images, one of which is probably right for your needs.

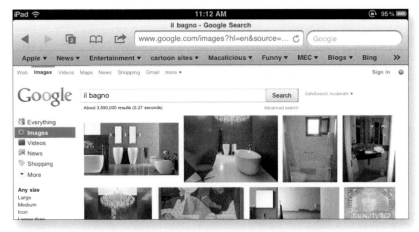

4. Tap an image that you think would make a good illustration.

   The image pops out of the page so that you can see it more clearly.

5. Tap the image again.

   Google displays a split screen, with the Web page on which the image appears on the left side and a set of display choices on the right side (**Figure 2.85**).

Figure 2.85 Google shows the image in context, along with information about the image and some additional options.

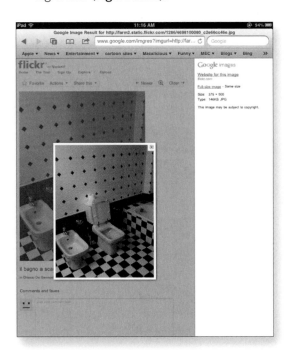

6. Tap the Full-size image link on the right side of the screen.

   The image appears by itself in Safari.

7. Tap and hold the image.

   Two option buttons appear (**Figure 2.86**).

Figure 2.86 You can save any image from the Web in your iPad's Photos app.

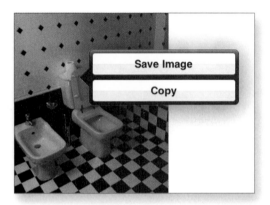

8. Tap Save Image.

   The image is saved in your iPad's Photos app. On an original iPad, you can find it in the Saved Photos album; on an iPad 2, it's in the Camera Roll album.

9. In the top-left corner of the Safari screen, tap the Back navigation button twice.

   The Google Images search results reappear. Notice the search field at the top of the results page. (You can see it in Figure 2.84 earlier in this project.) You'll use this field to perform additional image searches.

10. Delete the current keyword in the search field, search for *name tag,* and save a suitable image from the search results.

11. Search for *photography,* and choose and save a suitable image.

12. Search for, choose, and save an image of the Italian flag.

13. Press the iPad's Home button to close Safari.

note **Even when you close Safari, it keeps the pages you've been viewing in memory, so the translations you made earlier won't be lost. In fact, you'll use them again later in this project.**

Create your flash-card deck

Now that you've gathered all the text and images you need, you're ready to create your flash-card deck with Keynote.

Keep in mind as you work through this section that Keynote automatically saves all your additions and changes, so you can leave and come back to Keynote without worrying about saving your work or losing your place.

 Keynote works only in landscape orientation. If you turn your iPad to portrait orientation, Keynote remains in landscape orientation.

 A terminology note: Keynote creates and displays what it calls *slides*. Although we've been talking about flash cards, we'll use the term *slides* when we discuss flash cards in the context of Keynote.

Creating a new presentation:

1. Launch Keynote, and tap New Presentation in the top-left corner of the screen.

    The Choose a Theme screen appears (**Figure 2.87**).

Figure 2.87 Keynote offers you many presentation themes to choose among.

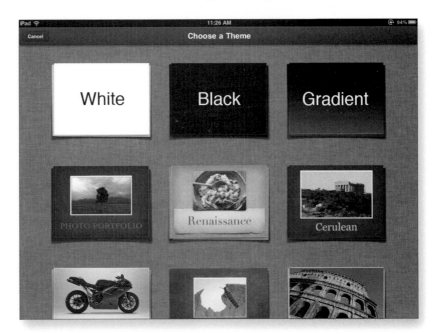

2. Tap the Renaissance theme.

A new presentation using the theme appears, displaying a placeholder image provided by that theme and two text fields (**Figure 2.88**). Tap a field to cut, copy, or delete it; double-tap a field to edit its contents.

Figure 2.88 The new presentation, with placeholder image and fields.

3. Double-tap the large text field below the picture, and type **Italian Words and Phrases**.

4. Tap the small text field at the bottom of the slide once to select it; then tap it again to produce a set of options (**Figure 2.89**).

Figure 2.89 Tap a selected field to cut, copy, or delete it.

5. You don't need the field at the bottom of the first slide, so tap Delete to get rid of it.

6. In the bottom-right corner of the placeholder picture in the center of the slide, tap the camera icon.

A Photo Albums popover appears (**Figure 2.90**).

Figure 2.90 Pick a picture from a photo album to put on the slide.

7. Tap Saved Photos (on an original iPad) or Camera Roll (on an iPad 2), swipe through the displayed photos until you see the Italian-flag image (which will be on your iPad if you completed the steps in "Gathering images with Google Images" earlier in this project), and then tap it.

   The Italian flag replaces the placeholder picture.

8. Drag the picture until it's centered on the slide above the text (**Figure 2.91**).

   Now that you have a title slide for the flash-card deck, you can use it to create the other slides.

Figure 2.91 The replacement picture is in place.

note   As you drag the picture, guidelines appear when the image approaches the center of the slide vertically or horizontally. Keynote provides these guidelines to help you place objects on a slide more precisely. When the guidelines appear, you can lift your finger; the picture snaps into place.

Duplicating and editing a slide:

1. In the column on the left side of the screen, tap the thumbnail of the slide to display the image-editing options (**Figure 2.92**).

Figure 2.92
Slide-editing options in Keynote.

The thumbnails in the left column show the order of slides in your presentation. You can drag them around, edit them, and skip them. If you have more than one slide, you have to tap an unselected slide once to select it and then tap it again to see its editing options. Because you have only one slide at this point, however, and it's selected, a single tap displays the options.

2. Tap Copy, tap the thumbnail again, and then tap Paste.

A second thumbnail appears in the column below the first, and its contents are displayed in Keynote's main viewing area. As you'd expect, this image is a duplicate of the first slide—for the moment.

3. Double-tap the text field on the slide, and enter the new text **Hello. My name is _____.**

4. Tap the picture once, pause, tap again to display the image-editing options (see the nearby sidebar "iPad Editing Techniques"), and then tap Replace.

You want to put a different picture on the slide, so you need to get rid of the existing one first. When you tap Replace, the Photo Albums popover appears.

5. Tap either Saved Photos (original iPad) or Camera Roll (iPad 2) and then tap the name-tag image (which will be on your iPad if you completed the steps in "Gathering images with Google Images" earlier in this project).

6. Drag the photo so that it's centered above the text field.

   You have the English version of a phrase slide. Next, you make the slide that has the Italian translation.

iPad Editing Techniques

When you begin editing a text field, you can use the common iPad editing tools:

- Tap to select a location in the text.

- Tap and hold to see a magnified view of the text and then drag to position the cursor.

- Double-tap a word to select it and then drag the selection handles to adjust the selection.

- Tap a selection or a location in the text to open the text-editing controls shown in **Figure 2.93**.

Figure 2.93
Editing options for a Keynote text field.

Making an Italian slide and completing the deck:

1. Follow steps 1–2 of the preceding task, "Duplicating and editing a slide," to make a duplicate of the English slide you just completed.

2. Double-click the iPad's Home button to display the apps panel at the bottom of the screen.

3. Tap the Safari icon to open Safari, tap the Pages button in Safari's toolbar, and then tap the thumbnail for the page of translated text that you created earlier in this project.

   You want to copy the Italian translation of the English text that currently appears on the duplicate slide.

4. Just to the right of the translated text, tap and hold the screen until a blue selection rectangle appears (**Figure 2.94**).

Figure 2.94 Selecting the text to copy.

 You tap and hold to the right of the translation because when you tap the text itself, Google helpfully supplies alternative translations for the text you tapped instead of selecting the text. Tapping beside the text selects the entire translated text area so that you can adjust your selection and then copy it.

5. Drag the blue control handles on the selected text until just the first sentence is selected; then tap Copy.

6. Double-click the Home button on your iPad; then tap the Keynote icon in the Recent apps panel at the bottom of the screen.

    The slide that you just duplicated is displayed.

7. Double-tap the text field to edit the text, select all the text, and then paste the Italian translation that's on the clipboard.

    The English text on the duplicated slide is replaced by the Italian translation. Now you have an Italian slide to match the English one. Next, you'll duplicate *this* slide and make it into the next English slide in the presentation.

8. Repeat all the steps in "Duplicating and editing a slide" earlier in this project, but with the following changes:

    In step 3, enter the second English phrase: **Where is the restroom?**

    In step 5, select the bathroom image.

9. Make an Italian slide by repeating steps 1–7 of this list.

10. Repeat steps 8–9 of this list, substituting the appropriate pictures and text (when you get to the step where you enter the English text, enter **Excuse me. Would you take a picture of us?**), to make the third set of slides.

Voila! You have a short flash-card presentation of Italian words and phrases. If you like, you can add to the presentation at any time.

Viewing the presentation:

1. In the thumbnail column on the left side of the Keynote screen, tap the topmost thumbnail.

This thumbnail represents the title slide that you made in "Creating a new presentation" earlier in this project. Keynote displays the title slide in the main work area.

2. Tap the Play button in the top-right corner.

The slide expands to fill the entire screen.

3. Tap anywhere on the slide.

The next slide is displayed.

4. Continue to tap until the last slide is displayed.

5. Tap the last slide.

Tapping the last slide ends the presentation and displays the slide-composition screen again.

Now that your flash-card composition is complete, it's ready to share. Naturally, you can share it simply by using your iPad to display it, but if you want to give it to someone, you need to export it or print it.

 You can double-tap a presentation at any time to return to the slide-composition screen.

 To print from an iPad, you must have an AirPrint-capable printer on a Wi-Fi network to which the iPad is connected. To find out more about AirPrint, see www.apple.com/ipad/features/airprint.html.

Printing the flash cards:

1. Tap the Tools button near the right end of the Keynote toolbar to see the Tools popover (**Figure 2.95**).

Figure 2.95
Tools popover.

Tools button

2. In the Tools popover, tap Print.

   The Printer Options popover appears.

3. Tap Printer to open the Printer popover, which shows the AirPrint printers on your Wi-Fi network.

4. Tap a printer to select it and then tap Printer options to return to the Printer Options popover.

5. Set the printing options, if necessary (**Figure 2.96**).

Figure 2.96 Use the Printer Options popover to specify what gets printed and on which printer.

The printing options include the range of pages to print and the number of copies to print.

6. Tap the Print button.

Exporting the flash cards:

1. In the top-left corner of the Keynote screen, tap My Presentations.

   Keynote displays the available presentations, with a large thumbnail of the flash-card presentation centered onscreen. You need to rename the presentation, because it currently has a generic name (such as Presentation 1).

2. Tap the presentation's name, delete the existing name in the editable title field that appears, and type a new name.

3. Tap the thumbnail to complete the renaming.

4. Tap the Action button (the leftmost button at the bottom of the screen).

   A dialog offers you several choices:

   - You can send the presentation via email. If you choose this option, you can send a Keynote file or a PDF version of that file.

   - You can share the presentation on the iWork.com site so that other people can download a copy, and you can share it as a Keynote file or a PDF. When you choose this option, Keynote creates an email with download information that you can send to your intended recipients.

   - You can export the presentation in either Keynote or PDF format to your iPad's file-sharing area and then use iTunes to copy the file from your iPad to your computer. We explain this process in the **Go to Meeting Project** earlier in this chapter.

   - You can copy the presentation to your MobileMe iDisk if you subscribe to MobileMe.

   - You can copy the presentation to a WebDAV server if you have access to such a server.

5. Tap the option of your choice, and follow the onscreen instructions.

Vacation Planning Project

Difficulty level: Easy

Software needed: KAYAK HD (free), TravelTracker ($2.99)

iPad models: Any

Additional hardware: None

The whole point of a vacation is to get away from the stress of daily life. Ironically, most vacations begin with the stress of planning the vacation: picking the dates; planning the itinerary; and then (one of the biggest stressors of them all) dancing the airline online tango, which can involve stepping from one airline Web site to another, searching for a flight that you can afford but that doesn't involve three intermediate stops and a 3 a.m. departure time.

In this project, you use two apps that help ameliorate the stress of getting away to be unstressed. With them, you can find the right flights and manage the trivia of planning your voyage away from it all—or almost all, because you're going to take your iPad with you, right?

Don't forget the charger.

Pack your apps

The first app you need is TravelTracker. This app has existed in one form or another since back in the 20th century, when Apple made the proto-iPad that it called the Newton. Through many incarnations, it has helped travelers track their traveling trivia: the itineraries, the frequent-flyer miles accrued, the places to visit, the stuff to pack, the things to do, and the places to stay. No, it won't magically handle all these things for you—you still have to enter these bits of information into the app—but it keeps them in one place, easily available and nicely arranged.

The second app is KAYAK (technically called KAYAK HD in the iTunes Store). This app, and the associated KAYAK Web site for which the app is a convenient front end, links with most major airlines. With it, you can search for flight information, and pick the flights that fit your budget and your traveling preferences.

The icons for the apps are shown in **Figure 2.97**. Go and get them.

Figure 2.97 The two apps you need for this project.

Getting the apps:

1. Purchase the inexpensive TravelTracker app from the App Store, either directly on your iPad or via iTunes on your computer.

    You can enter the following URL in your computer's Web browser to have it open iTunes and take you right to the download page:

    http://itunes.apple.com/us/app/traveltracker-personal-travel/id284918921?mt=8

2. Download the free KAYAK app from the App Store, either directly on your iPad or via iTunes on your computer.

    Enter the following URL in your computer's Web browser to have it open iTunes to the app's page in the App Store:

    http://itunes.apple.com/us/app/kayak-explore-flight-search/id363205965?mt=8

Set up a trip with TravelTracker

To set up a trip in TravelTracker, you need (of course) a trip to set up. For the purposes of this project, we're going to make up a trip just so we have something to illustrate when we walk you through the steps. Feel free to use your own trip details, if you prefer, substituting your entries for what we show here.

Our imaginary trip is from Los Angeles to Portland, Oregon, for the week of Thanksgiving. The visit starts on November 21, 2011, and ends on November 28, 2011. (If you're reading this book after those dates, you'll need to adjust the dates accordingly.) Near the end of the trip, we'll plan a post-Thanksgiving dinner at an exclusive restaurant to thank our hosts for putting us up.

In this part of the project, you create a new trip and schedule the dinner.

Creating a new trip:

1. Launch the TravelTracker app on your iPad.

   The first time you open the app, it provides a helpful tip, as shown in **Figure 2.98**. The app tells you about the screen you're looking at and mentions another service, TripIt, that makes TravelTracker even more useful. We won't use TripIt in this project, but it's worth checking out.

Figure 2.98
The All Trips page in TravelTracker, complete with a tip.

2. If the tip appears, tap OK to dismiss it; then tap the New Trip button in the top-right corner of the screen.

   A popover containing a New Trip form appears (**Figure 2.99**). Note that the form starts the trip on the current date. You need to change that date, but first, you should give the trip a name.

Figure 2.99 Creating a new trip.

Figure 2.99 Creating a new trip.

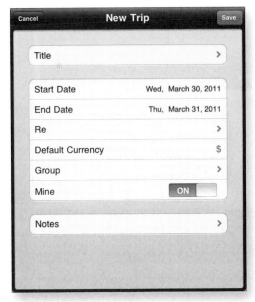

3. In the form, tap Title.

   An Edit Trip Name form appears.

4. Type a title, such as **Holiday In Portland** (**Figure 2.100**).

Figure 2.100 Every trip needs a name.

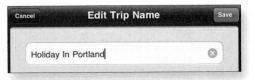

5. Tap the Save button in the top-right corner to save your work and close the form.

   The New Trip form returns.

6. Tap Start Date.

   An Edit Trip Dates form opens, featuring a standard iPad date-selection widget.

7. Tap the Start field, and use the widget to dial the start date—for this project, November 21, 2011.

   Your selected date appears in the Start field (**Figure 2.101** on the next page).

Figure 2.101 Select
your trip dates with the
date-dialing widget.

8. Tap the End field, and use the widget to dial the end date—for this
   project, November 28, 2011.

   The selected end date appears in the End field.

9. Tap Save in the top-right corner to save your work and close the form.

   The New Trip Form returns.

10. Tap Save.

   The trip is saved, and you see a blank itinerary screen for the
   Holiday In Portland trip (or whatever you called the trip you just
   created), as shown in **Figure 2.102**.

Figure 2.102
The Holiday In Portland
trip has a blank itiner-
ary for now.

If you're using TravelTracker for the first time, a help tip explains the itinerary screen that you just created. This itinerary screen holds various items for your trip, such as flights, planned meals, and lodging—or *will* hold these items when you create them. Right now, it's stunningly empty.

It's time to put something in your itinerary. Something tasty.

 You can buy add-ons that expand TravelTracker's capabilities. One such add-on, which currently costs 99 cents, provides checklists for items to pack and pretrip tasks to perform (such as stopping mail delivery). If you find yourself worrying about whether you remembered to start the dishwasher as you stand in line waiting to board, that add-on may be just what you need.

Scheduling a dinner:

1. In the top-right corner of the itinerary screen (refer to Figure 2.102), tap New Item.

    The New Item popover displays a list of items that you can add to the itinerary (**Figure 2.103**).

Figure 2.103 Any or all of these items can go in your itinerary.

2. Tap Dining.

   A New Dining screen appears (**Figure 2.104**). This screen, where you add restaurant and reservation information, sets the reservation to the first day of the trip by default. The time is also set by default to 6 p.m.; you won't need to change it for this task. (After all, 6 p.m. is a good time for dinner.)

Figure 2.104 Enter information about your dining plans here.

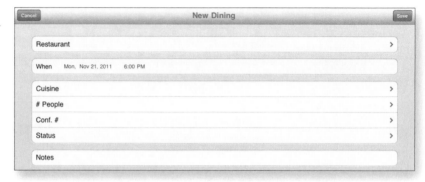

3. Tap the When field.

   A date-and-time-selection widget appears, displaying the default date and time (**Figure 2.105**).

Figure 2.105 Set this widget so that you won't miss dinner.

4. Set the date to November 26 and then tap Save.

   You return to the New Dining screen.

5. Tap the Restaurant field.

   A blank Edit Name screen appears (**Figure 2.106**).

Figure 2.106
In TravelTracker, the restaurant name includes phone, address, city, and country as well.

6. Tap each field, and enter some appropriate information (using a real restaurant or just making something up).

   If you happen to have the restaurant in your iPad's Contacts app, you can tap the blue plus sign (+) at the right end of the Name field to add the restaurant's name, address, phone number, and city to the Edit Name screen. If you don't, you can enter each item manually.

7. Tap Save to save your work and close the Edit Name screen.

   The New Dining screen reappears, with the restaurant information filled in.

8. (Optional) Tap each field in the New Dining screen, and enter information for each one.

   A typical New Dining screen looks like **Figure 2.107** when it's filled out.

Figure 2.107 Dinner at an exclusive restaurant, ready to be added to your itinerary.

9. Tap Save.

   Your itinerary now has a dining item scheduled (**Figure 2.108**).

Figure 2.108 At last, your itinerary has something in it.

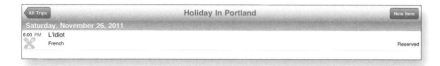

10. Press your iPad's Home button to exit TravelTracker.

    It's time to move to KAYAK and schedule a flight.

Find flights with KAYAK

As you may have noticed in TravelTracker, you can add flights to your itinerary. Before you can do that, though, you have to have some flights to add. You use KAYAK to find those flights and even book them.

 The flight information shown in this section is subject to change and is shown only for example purposes. No endorsement of particular airlines is intended.

Setting flight routes with KAYAK:

1. Launch the KAYAK app on your iPad.

   KAYAK opens, showing you its main screen.

2. In the Flight Search pane on the left side of the screen, tap the From field.

   A Choose Origin Airport pane appears next to the Flight Search pane (**Figure 2.109**).

Figure 2.109 Use the Choose Origin Airport pane to search for the airport from which you want to depart.

3. In the search field at the top of the pane, begin typing **Los Angeles**.

    As you type, airport abbreviations begin to appear below the search field. As soon as you see *LAX,* you can stop typing (**Figure 2.110**).

Figure 2.110 KAYAK knows about a lot of airports.

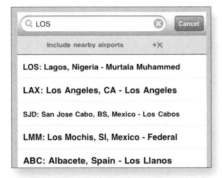

tip **Alternatively, you can tap Current Location in the Choose Origin Airport pane (refer to Figure 2.109) to have KAYAK list the airports in your general area.**

4. Tap LAX in the list of airports that appears.

    The origin airport you selected appears in the From field of the Flight Search pane.

5. At the top of the Flight Search pane, tap Round Trip if it isn't already selected.

6. In the Flight Search pane, tap the To location, and in the Choose Destination Airport pane that appears, begin to type **Portland, Oregon** (**Figure 2.111**).

Figure 2.111 Pick a destination airport.

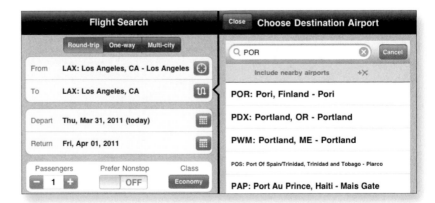

7. When *PDX* (the airport in Portland, Oregon) appears in the pane, tap that entry; then tap Close at the top of the screen.

In the Flight Search pane, PDX is listed as the destination.

Next, you'll set the travel dates and search for a flight.

Setting travel dates and finding a flight:

1. In the Flight Search pane (refer to Figure 2.109), tap the Depart field to open the Choose Depart Date pane.

2. Swipe down the Choose Depart Date form to November, and tap 21 on the calendar (**Figure 2.112**).

Figure 2.112 KAYAK uses calendars instead of date-dialing widgets.

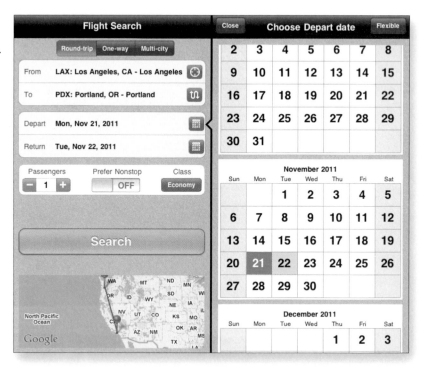

3. In the Flight Search pane, tap the Return field to open the Choose Return Date pane to the right.

4. Swipe down the Choose Return Date pane, and tap November 28; then tap the Close button.

5. Back in the Flight Search pane, find the Passengers indicator; tap the + button to increase the number of passengers to 2; tap the Prefer Nonstop switch to turn that setting on; and tap the Class button if you want to choose a flight class other than Economy (**Figure 2.113**).

Figure 2.113 Set the number of passengers, and tell KAYAK whether you want to go non-stop and what class you want to travel in.

6. Tap the big orange Search button above the map (refer to Figure 2.112).

    KAYAK displays the flight search results.

7. Swipe up and down the search results to find a suitable flight, and when you do, tap it.

    The Flight Details pane appears on the right side of the screen, with a Booking pane below it (**Figure 2.114**).

Figure 2.114 Click a link or make a phone call to book the flight that you've chosen.

At this point, you can call one of the listed numbers or click a link in the Booking pane to book your flight. Because this task is just an example, however, make a note of the airlines and the flight numbers so that you can use them in the next section.

If you like, you can tap and hold the text in the Flight Details pane to see text-selection controls. You can use these controls to select all the flight detail information and copy it to the iPad's clipboard so that you can paste it into another document for reference.

8. Press the iPad's Home button to exit the KAYAK app.

Add flight information to your itinerary

Now that you have your flight information, you can add your departure and return flights to your TravelTracker itinerary.

Entering flight information with TravelTracker:

1. Launch TravelTracker on your iPad again.

   You see your itinerary screen just as you left it (refer to Figure 2.108).

2. Tap New Item in the top-right corner to open the New Item form.

3. Tap Flight.

   The New Flight screen appears (**Figure 2.115**).

Figure 2.115 The New Flight screen holds a lot of information about your flight, and TravelTracker helps you fill it out.

4. Tap the Airline field at the top of the screen.

   The Select Airline screen appears (**Figure 2.116**).

Figure 2.116 Select an airline.

5. Find the airline for your departure flight, and tap it.

In the unlikely event that your airline isn't listed in the Select Airline screen, tap the Add Other Airline button in the bottom-left corner and then follow the onscreen instructions to add it.

The New Flight screen reappears.

6. Tap the Flight # field to open the Edit Flight # screen.

7. Type the flight number (**Figure 2.117**), and tap Save.

Figure 2.117 The flight-number field can hold a *very* long flight number.

The New Flight screen returns briefly but is quickly replaced by the Departure Date screen, which contains a date-selection widget.

8. If the departure date for this project—November 21, 2011—isn't already selected, use the widget to dial it in and then tap Save.

TravelTracker looks up the flight and fills out the rest of the form, as shown in **Figure 2.118**.

Figure 2.118 TravelTracker fills out the rest of the New Flight form as soon as it has an airline, a flight number, and a date.

9. Tap Save.

The departure flight appears in your itinerary screen.

10. Repeat steps 2–9, using the return-flight number, the airline, and the return date that you got from your KAYAK search (assuming that you completed both tasks in "Find flights with KAYAK" earlier in this project).

Your itinerary now contains your departure flight, your return flight, and your dinner information (**Figure 2.119**).

Figure 2.119
Your itinerary is start-ing to look useful.

11. Press the iPad's Home button to exit TravelTracker.

The beginnings of your vacation plan are stored in TravelTracker, with an assist from KAYAK. Have a great trip! Remember to drop us a postcard!

3

Music, Books, and Movies on the iPad

In the preceding chapter, we take issue with the conventional notion that the iPad is just a media-consumption device. We think that we prove our point.

Nonetheless, the iPad really is a delightful media-consumption device if you want to use it as one. The trick is getting the media you want on it, when you want it, and in the form that you want it. This chapter shows you those tricks.

Our philosophy is this: If you're a consumer, you owe it to yourself to be the best consumer that you can be.

Make Music Project

Difficulty level: Easy

Software needed: GarageBand for iPad ($4.99)

iPad model: Any

Additional hardware: None

Whether or not you think that calling the iPad "magical" is an egregious example of marketing exaggeration, the first time you start to play with Apple's GarageBand app, you may find that the adjective gains credibility.

Think of it: a home recording studio that fits into a wafer-thin slab of glass and metal, and that's priced lower than a burger and fries. Not only that, but also, it's a recording studio equipped with musical instruments that know how to play themselves. GarageBand may not be magical, but it'll do until Merlin drops by with his psaltery for a jam session.

In this project, you use GarageBand's Smart Instruments to compose and record a simple song.

Obtain the GarageBand app

If you're a Mac owner, chances are that you've already seen the Mac version of GarageBand, which has shipped with every new Mac for years as part of Apple's iLife software suite. Recently, Apple has made it available for separate purchase from the Mac App Store. You don't need a Mac or the Mac version of GarageBand to use the GarageBand app on your iPad, however. All you need are an iPad and $4.99.

Getting the app:

* Purchase the GarageBand app from the App Store, either directly on your iPad or via iTunes on your computer.

    Figure 3.1 shows its icon.

Figure 3.1 The icon for GarageBand.

You can enter the following URL in your computer's Web browser to have it open iTunes and take you right to the download page:

http://itunes.apple.com/us/app/garageband/id408709785?mt=8

Set up a song

When you open a newly installed copy of GarageBand, it creates a new song for you and shows you the Instruments screen (**Figure 3.2**). If you see anything else, you need to create a new song yourself.

Figure 3.2
The Instruments screen, where you pick an instrument to play and record.

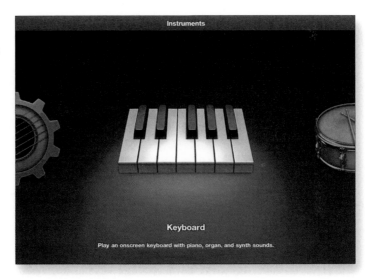

Here's what you may see when you open a previously used GarageBand app:

- The My Songs screen, showing the songs you've created so far

- The My Songs screen, telling you that no songs have been created yet

- An incomplete song on which you've been working

Starting a new song:

1. Open the GarageBand app.

2. Do one of the following things:

   - If you see the My Songs screen, which shows one or more existing songs, tap the New Song button at the bottom of the screen and then tap New Song in the popover (**Figure 3.3** on the next page).

Figure 3.3 Making a new song when you have other songs available.

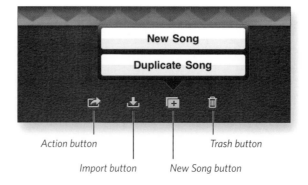

Action button

Import button

New Song button

Trash button

- If you see an empty My Songs screen (**Figure 3.4**), tap the center of the screen to start a new song.

Figure 3.4 The My Songs screen when you haven't created a song yet.

No songs exist in the My Songs browser
Tap here to start a new song.

- If you see a song screen of some sort, tap the My Songs button in the top-left left corner (**Figure 3.5**); then tap the New Song icon at the bottom of the My Songs screen, and tap New Song in the popover (refer to Figure 3.3).

Figure 3.5 The My Songs button takes you to the My Songs screen from within a song.

- If you see the Instruments screen (refer to Figure 3.2), take a deep breath: The new song has already been created, and you're ready for the next step.

At this point, no matter what you saw when you opened the app, you should see the Instruments screen. Now you're ready to choose an instrument to play.

Picking a guitar:

1. On the Instruments screen, scroll to the left until you see the Smart Guitar and then tap it.

   The Smart Guitar instrument screen appears (**Figure 3.6**). Here, you can choose a different kind of guitar, adjust the key and tempo, and set other options. Most important, the Smart Guitar is preset with various chords that harmonize, ready for you to play without hitting a wrong note!

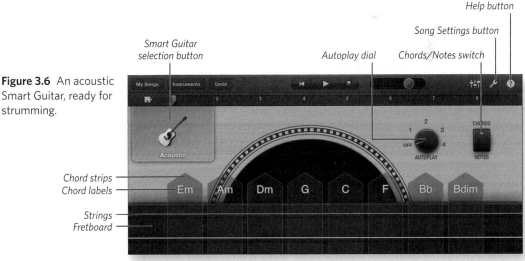

Figure 3.6 An acoustic Smart Guitar, ready for strumming.

Help button

Song Settings button

Smart Guitar selection button

Autoplay dial   *Chords/Notes switch*

Chord strips
Chord labels

Strings
Fretboard

tip   **Tap the Help button in the top-right corner to see helpful tags that describe what various parts of the Smart Guitar screen do. You can continue play when the help tags are visible.**

2. Make sure that the Chords/Notes switch is set to Chords and then strum various chord strips to hear what they sound like.

To strum, swipe up or down in a chord strip.

3. Tap a few strings in various chord strips to hear how they sound when played individually.

4. Tap the chord label above a chord strip.

   Tapping a chord label plays the complete chord.

Autoplaying your guitar:

1. In the ring of numbers around the Autoplay dial (refer to Figure 3.6), tap 1.

   The Autoplay dial indicator points to 1, and the strings vanish from the guitar fretboard (**Figure 3.7**).

Figure 3.7 Setting Autoplay to 1 makes the strings vanish— but that's a *good* thing.

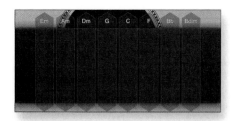

2. Tap any chord strip with a single finger.

   You hear the chord strummed in a rhythmic pattern.

3. Tap the same chord strip with two fingers.

   The strum pattern changes.

4. Tap the same chord strip with three fingers.

   The strum pattern changes slightly again.

5. Tap the 2 above the Autoplay dial and listen for a moment; tap 3 and listen for a moment; and then tap 4.

   You hear a finger-picking rhythm. Each time you tap a number, the rhythm changes.

6. Tap the chord strip that's currently playing with a single finger.

   The playing stops.

note As you've just seen and heard, each number on the Autoplay dial provides three different strumming and finger-picking patterns for each chord, depending on the number of fingers with which you tap a chord strip. All told, you can choose among 12 Autoplay patterns for each Smart Guitar chord.

Prepare to record

With GarageBand, you can record songs with up to eight tracks. By default, you record each track in eight-bar sections. If you don't know what a bar is, don't worry; you don't have to know. By some strange coincidence, each strumming and picking pattern (refer to "Autoplaying your guitar" earlier in this project) lasts for one bar before it repeats.

In this part of the project, you use those patterns to your advantage. You record an eight-bar selection of chords, using four chords and playing each chord pattern twice. When you finish, you'll end up with a portion of a song that probably sounds familiar to you, because it's been used in several songs over the years.

First, though, you need to set up the tempo (how fast the patterns play, in number of beats per minute). You also set up a metronome count-in so that you can become familiar with the tempo before you start playing.

Setting up the recording:

1. In the top-right corner of the Smart Guitar screen, tap the Song Settings button to open the Song Settings popover (**Figure 3.8**).

Figure 3.8 Use the Song Settings popover to set the metronome, song tempo, and song key.

2. Make sure that the Metronome and Count-In switches are both set to On.

The metronome plays a click or tap for each beat. Because each bar lasts four beats by default (you can change this setting but won't for this project), it plays four clicks per bar for this task. When Count-In is on, the metronome plays one bar of beats before the recording begins so that you have time to get ready to play.

3. In the Tempo section of the popover, tap slowly and steadily in the Tap to set Tempo box so that the Tempo indicator (which displays beats per minute) displays 80.

The faster you tap, the higher the number in the Tempo indicator and the faster the song plays. You want a slow tempo to make recording easier. You can change the song's tempo later—as, in fact, you will in "Resetting the tempo" later in this project.

Tap the arrows in the Tempo indicator to fine-tune the setting so that it's exactly 80. Tapping the up arrow increases the tempo, and tapping the down arrow decreases it.

You don't need to change the other settings in the Song Settings popover: Sound, which changes the sound of the metronome, and Key, which changes the key in which the chords are set (by default, C major).

Recording a track

When you make a recording or play it back, a playhead moves across the control bar at the top of the screen (**Figure 3.9**). Pay attention to the playhead: it shows you where you are in the recording. You can drag the playhead around with your finger to move it to different parts of the recording. While you're recording, the duration appears in red on the timeline; when you've completed the recording, the duration appears in green on the timeline.

Centered above the timeline and playhead are the transport controls: Go to Beginning/Stop, Play, and Record. You tap the transport controls to position the playhead at the beginning of the song section, start or stop playback, and begin recording.

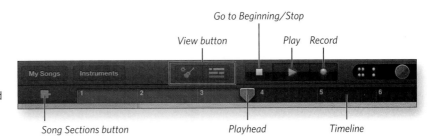

Figure 3.9
The playhead and transport controls. Red indicates the recording's progress.

In the following task, you record a take.

We recommend that you read the steps first to become familiar with what you'll do and the chords you'll play. You may even want to do a run-through or two before you begin recording.

Doing a take:

1. Tap the Go to Beginning/Stop transport control to set the playhead at the far-left end of the timeline (refer to Figure 3.9).

    Recording begins at the playhead position, and you want to begin at the beginning.

2. Set the Autoplay dial to 2.

    This setting gives you a nice folksy finger-picking rhythm.

3. Tap the red Record transport control.

    GarageBand begins the count-in (which you set in "Setting up the recording" earlier in this project).

4. Following the fourth count-in beat, tap the C (C major) chord strip (refer to Figure 3.6 earlier in this project) with a single finger.

5. As soon as the finger-picking rhythm has played twice (and the playhead is approaching the bar 3 mark in the timeline), tap the Am (A minor) chord strip.

6. At the end of two A-minor repetitions, when the playhead is approaching the bar 5 mark in the timeline, tap the Dm (D minor) chord strip.

7. At the end of two D-minor repetitions, when the playhead is coming up on the bar 7 mark in the timeline, tap the G (G major) chord strip.

When the playhead reaches the end of the song segment, GarageBand automatically stops recording and immediately begins to play back what it just recorded.

8. Listen to your recording.

If you don't like your recording, don't worry. Just repeat these steps to erase the recording and redo it. You won't be charged for extra studio time.

 note **You hear the metronome during playback, but it's not part of the recording. If the sound bothers you, tap the Song Settings button to open the Song Settings popover (refer to Figure 3.8) and then tap the Metronome switch to turn it off.**

Adding a new instrument in a new section:

 1. In the control bar, to the left of the transport controls, tap the View button.

The screen changes to show GarageBand's track view (**Figure 3.10**). You use this view to add or remove song sections, add or remove instrument tracks, and arrange your recordings.

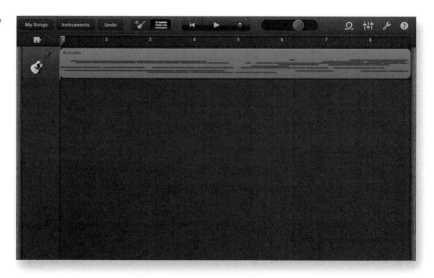

Figure 3.10 Track view shows the instrument tracks and the recordings in your song.

Currently, your song has one instrument track and one eight-bar section. The big green area below the control bar is the Acoustic Smart Guitar recording region that you created in the preceding section.

All recordings you make are stored in regions, which you can edit and move around (as you will in "Looping a region" later in this project).

2. At the left end of the control bar, tap the Song Sections button (refer to Figure 3.9) to bring up the Song Sections popover (**Figure 3.11**).

Figure 3.11 Use the Song Sections popover to add or remove sections and to choose which sections are displayed.

3. In the popover, tap the Add button.

A new section appears in the popover (**Figure 3.12**). You may notice that the track view now shows more bars for the moment.

Figure 3.12 A new section has been added to the song.

4. Tap anywhere outside the popover.

The popover goes away, and the track view shows bars 9–16. The Smart Guitar track is empty because you haven't yet recorded those bars.

5. In the bottom-left corner of the track-view screen, tap the plus sign (+) to add a new instrument track.

You see the same Instruments screen that you saw early in this project (refer to Figure 3.2).

6. As you did earlier, scroll left and choose Smart Guitar.

   You see the same Smart Guitar screen shown in Figure 3.6 earlier in this project.

7. Tap the Smart Guitar selection button to see the available guitars (**Figure 3.13**).

Figure 3.13 A choice of Smart Guitars.

8. Tap the Rock Roots guitar.

   The Smart Guitar screen updates to reflect your choice.

   Although the Roots Rock screen looks different from the Acoustic screen and has a couple of new features (to be precise, two stompbox effects that you can turn on to change the sound of the guitar), the new guitar operates much like the acoustic one that you've been playing.

9. Switch the Autoplay dial to 3 (**Figure 3.14**).

Figure 3.14 A new look for a new guitar.

10. Tap the Go to Beginning/Stop transport control (refer to Figure 3.9) to set the playhead at the far-left end of the timeline.

11. Complete steps 3–8 of "Doing a take" earlier in this project to record the new song segment in the Roots Rock guitar track.

    You'll notice that the Roots Rock Smart Guitar has a distinctly different sound and Autoplay pattern from the Acoustic Smart Guitar. Also, the count-in includes the final bar of the first song section.

12. If you muffed the take, repeat steps 10–11 to redo it.

Arrange the recording

The two recordings you've made are a good start. Now you get a chance to fill out the arrangement.

In the following sections, you perform several tasks:

- Make one of your recordings loop.

- Add a drum track.

- Reset the tempo to give your song a livelier feel.

Looping a region:

1. Switch back to the track-view screen (refer to Figure 3.10 earlier in this project).

2. Tap the Song Sections button at the left end of the timeline to open the Song Sections popover.

3. Tap the All Sections button.

4. Tap anywhere in the track-view screen to dismiss the Song Sections popover.

5. Tap the Acoustic Smart Guitar region to select it; then tap that region again to display the editing controls (**Figure 3.15**).

Figure 3.15 Editing controls for a selected region.

6. In the editing-controls bar, tap Loop.

   The Acoustic Smart Guitar region expands to fill the entire track (**Figure 3.16**).

Figure 3.16
A looped region.

You can loop any of GarageBand's built-in instruments to create repetitions of a recording. In this case, the eight bars you recorded with the Acoustic Smart Guitar are repeated again for bars 9–16.

Adding a drum track:

1. Tap the Loop button near the top-right corner of the track-view screen to open the Apple Loops popover (**Figure 3.17**).

Figure 3.17
Apple Loops contains hundreds of tasty recorded loops.

Loop button

You can preview a loop simply by tapping it. You can also narrow the selection of loops by tapping the Instrument, Genre, and Descriptors options near the top of the popover and then tapping the kinds of loops you want to see. If you know the name of the loop that you want to use, however, you can search for it.

For this task, you want to use a drum loop called Solid 70s Fill 23.

2. Tap the search field at the top of the Apple Loops popover to display an onscreen keyboard; then type **solid** and tap Search on the keyboard.

   The popover now displays a much shorter list of loops, all of which have *solid* in their names.

3. Find the Solid 70s Fill 23 loop in the popover, and drag it to the left side of the track-view screen, below the Acoustic and Roots Rock Smart Guitar icons.

   As you drag, a new track appears, filled with the loop.

4. Lift your finger off the screen.

   The drum track spans the entire song (**Figure 3.18**).

Figure 3.18
A prerecorded drum loop has been added to the song.

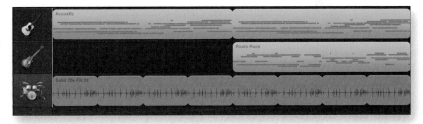

Resetting the tempo:

1. Tap the Song Settings button to open the Song Settings popover (refer to Figure 3.8 earlier in this project).

2. In the Tempo section, use the Tempo controls to set the tempo to 110.

   For details on setting the tempo, refer to "Setting up the recording" earlier in this project.

3. Set the Metronome switch to Off.

4. Tap outside the Song Settings popover to dismiss it.

5. Tap the Play transport control to play your finished song.

    The song plays faster, with an added drum track, and the acoustic guitar plays along with the rock guitar in the last eight bars.

    Congratulations—you're an iPad recording artist!

Share your performance

A recording artist needs an audience, and GarageBand makes it easy for you to reach yours. You can save your song to iTunes or email it to your fans. The iTunes option makes a copy of your song that you can access via iTunes File Sharing when you connect your iPad to your computer. In the following sections, we show you how to use both distribution methods.

Saving to iTunes:

1. In the top-left corner of the track-view screen, tap the My Songs button.

    The My Songs screen appears, displaying the song you just finished.

2. Tap the Action button at the bottom of the screen to see your distribution choices (**Figure 3.19**).

Figure 3.19 Choose an export method for your song.

Action button

3. Tap Send to iTunes.

    The Choose Format window opens (**Figure 3.20**). You have two choices in this window:

    •   **iTunes:** This option creates an AAC file that you can play in iTunes on a computer or on an iPad, iPod, or any other device that can play AAC recordings. (Most modern music players can play them.)

    •   **GarageBand:** This option creates a GarageBand file that you can open in the Mac version of GarageBand.

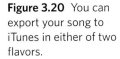

Figure 3.20 You can export your song to iTunes in either of two flavors.

4. Tap a format to export the song to your iPad.

   You can access the song via iTunes File Sharing when your iPad is connected to your computer.

Mailing your music:

1. In the My Songs screen, tap the Action button to open the popover (refer to Figure 3.19) and then tap Email Song.

   A mail message appears, with your song file (in AAC format) attached to it.

2. Address your message, add any other information you want, and then send it.

   All you have to do now is wait for your fans to line up for your next concert.

Music Syncing Project

Difficulty level: Easy

Software needed: iTunes (Mac or Windows)

iPad model: Any

Additional hardware: Mac or PC

More than a year into the iPad era, most technology pundits have finally moved on from the blithe critique stated so often at the device's intro-duction: "It's nothing but a giant iPod touch!"

In fact, though, this facile critique has some basis. Setting aside the iPad's unique capabilities, it *does* have much in common with the iPod touch. In particular, your iPad has a built-in iPod that you can use to play the thousands of songs your iPad can hold.

To act in its secret identity as a giant iPod touch, however, your iPad needs songs to play. If you're among the ever-shrinking number of souls who've never had an iPod—or even if you have one but find the whole music-syncing thing to be mystifying—this project shows you how to get the songs you want, by the artists you want, in the styles you want, from your iTunes Library to your plus-size iPod touch.

Sync everything

If you have a relatively small iTunes Library (that is, one that can fit easily into your particular iPad's storage space), deciding what music to put on your iPad is simple: Just put your whole Music library on the device, and don't worry about it. Even the smallest-capacity iPad has ample room to hold several thousand songs.

 Apple provides a ballpark estimate of about 250 songs per gigabyte. Going by that estimate, a 16 GB iPad can store 4,000 songs and still have a third of its storage space left for documents, pictures, apps, and other stuff.

Assuming that your Music library fits on your iPad, getting it there is just a few clicks and a sync away.

Making Smaller Songs to Save Space

Songs can be stored in various formats, some of which take up more space than others do. To conserve iPad storage space, do the following

1. With your iPad selected in iTunes' Source list, click the Summary button at the top of the main pane.

2. Near the bottom of the pane, select the option titled Convert higher bit rate songs to 128 kbps AAC.

This option increases the time that it takes to sync your music, because iTunes must convert every song that isn't in 128 Kbps AAC format as it syncs. Also, the process slightly reduces the sound quality of the synced songs on your iPad. But unless you have very-high-quality speakers or headphones attached to your iPad (and very good ears), you won't be able to tell the difference in the converted songs' sound quality.

Syncing your entire Music library to your iPad:

1. Connect your iPad to your computer.

2. Launch iTunes, if it doesn't launch automatically.

3. In the Source list on the left side of the iTunes window, select your iPad.

4. Click the Music button at the top of the main pane of the iTunes window.

   The contents of the music syncing pane for your iPad appear, with the main syncing options laid out at the top (**Figure 3.21**).

Figure 3.21 The main music syncing options for your iPad.

5. Select the Sync Music check box and the Entire music library radio button.

6. (Optional) Select Include music videos.

   Keep in mind that each music video takes up considerably more space than a typical song. But if you have the space (see the nearby sidebar), why not?

7. Click the Apply button in the bottom-right corner of the iTunes window.

   iTunes begins copying your entire Music library to your iPad. Depending on the size of the library and the speed of your computer, this process can take several minutes, so be patient; you have to do this only once. When you add more songs to your iTunes Library, only the additional songs will be copied to your iPad the next time you sync.

Sync artists and genres

If your iTunes Music library is too large for your iPad, or if you just don't want to copy the whole thing, you can narrow down which songs get synced in several ways. One of the easiest ways is to choose your favorite musical artists, musical genres, and albums, and then sync only the music that matches your choices.

iTunes presents the artists, genres, and albums associated with your songs in the music syncing pane for your iPad, right below the main music-syncing options (**Figure 3.22**). You use the check boxes in these lists to select your favorites.

Figure 3.22 The music syncing pane lists artists, genres, and albums.

Syncing selected artists and genres to your iPad:

1. Follow steps 1–3 of "Syncing your entire Music library to your iPad" earlier in this project.

2. Select the Sync Music check box and the radio button titled Selected playlists, artists, albums, and genres.

    The Playlists, Artists, Genres, and Albums lists become accessible so that you can check or clear the check boxes in them.

    We'll ignore the Playlists list for now, because we cover it in the next section of this project.

tip If some of the items in the Playlists list happen to be checked, you can easily clear all of them so that they don't interfere with this part of the project. To do so, hold down the Command (Mac) or Ctrl (Windows) key, and click one selected check-box item to deselect everything in the list. Similarly, clicking an unselected check box with the key held down selects every item in the list. This technique, by the way, works with almost every list in iTunes that has check boxes.

3. In the Artists list, select the artists whose songs you want to sync with your iPad.

4. In the Genres list, select the genres that you prefer.

note iTunes uses the genre assigned to the song by the vendor from which you obtained the song, such as the iTunes Store. It also uses information from an online database when you rip a CD to add its songs to your Music library. You can modify this information if you like; see the iTunes help topic "Edit Song and CD Information" to find out how.

5. In the Albums list, select the albums you want on your iPad.

6. Click Apply in the bottom-right corner of the iTunes window.

    iTunes syncs the songs that match your artist, album, and genre selections to your iPad, and removes any songs from your iPad that don't match your selections.

Make and sync playlists for your iPad

Some people who spend a lot of time with iTunes delight in arranging their songs in all sorts of ways by using iTunes' playlist features. Many other people, however, find playlists abstract and confusing, and shy away from them as though they were a nest of snakes.

If you're comfortable with playlists, simply skip to "Selecting and syncing playlists" later in this project. The rest of you, read on.

Playlists are actually quite simple: They're lists of one or more songs. That's it. They don't contain any actual songs—just references to songs. That's the part that seems to confuse people, because in iTunes, the act of adding songs to a playlist looks very much like copying the actual songs. It isn't. When you add songs to a playlist, you're simply adding *references* to those songs, as **Figure 3.23** illustrates.

Figure 3.23 It may *look* like we're copying four songs into a playlist, but we're really copying references to those songs.

Think of a room full of people. You can make a list of everyone in the room, and you can make another list of, say, just the left-handed people in the room. The people themselves aren't cloned and embedded magically in your lists; the lists contain only references to the people. The people themselves stay in the room where they were all along.

Similarly, when you add a song from your iTunes Music library to a playlist, the song itself isn't copied to the playlist; it stays where it is, in your Music library. You can add the same song to as many playlists as you like, just as you can add the same person to as many lists as you like, but no matter how many times a person is added to a list or a song is added to a playlist, only one physical person or only one actual song is involved.

When you sync a playlist from iTunes to your iPad, iTunes checks the songs that are already on your iPad. If a song in the playlist is already there, iTunes doesn't copy it to your iPad; if it isn't, iTunes copies the song to your device. That way, you can sync as many playlists to your iPad as you want, and even if the same song appears in all those playlists, only one copy of that song goes from your Music library to your iPad.

Playlists appear in the Source list on the left side of the iTunes window. Over time, you may find that you've made dozens of playlists. You can shorten the Source list by creating folders where you can store various playlists.

When you sync playlists between iTunes and your iPad, you can choose individual playlists, folders full of playlists, or individual playlists inside folders.

 When you select a folder of playlists in iTunes and sync that playlist folder to your iPad, all the playlists inside that folder are synced to your iPad. The icons for the playlist folders on your iPad don't look much like folders, however; they look more like stacks of playlists.

In the following tasks, you create a folder for the playlists that you want to have on your iPad, create a playlist inside that folder, add songs to that playlist, and then sync everything. When you have these steps down, you can go through your iTunes Library at leisure and create playlists and folders for your iPad to suit your needs and desires.

Making a playlist and playlist folder in iTunes:

1. In the iTunes Source list, click Music.

    All your music in iTunes appears in a list (**Figure 3.24**).

Figure 3.24 The Music library lives near the top of the Source list.

 Before you can create a playlist or a playlist folder, iTunes must be displaying content from one of your libraries.

2. Choose File > New Playlist Folder.

A folder appears in the Playlists section of the Source list with its title selected, ready for you to edit it (**Figure 3.25**).

Figure 3.25 A new playlist folder awaiting its new name.

3. Type a folder name, and press Return (Mac) or Enter (Windows).

For this task, type **iPad songs**. When you press Return or Enter, the folder is renamed. If your Playlist section contains other folders, they appear in alphabetical order, and the newly named folder moves to its correct alphabetical position among them.

4. Click the new folder to select it and then choose File > New Playlist.

An untitled playlist appears inside the folder, ready for you to rename it.

5. Type a new name for the playlist (whatever name you like), and press Return or Enter.

6. Add songs to your new playlist.

You can add songs to a playlist whether that playlist is in a folder or not, of course, but putting playlists inside folders makes it more convenient to sync them with your iPad. In this project, you're using only one playlist, but you can use the folder you just created to contain all the playlists destined for your iPad.

tip You can drag any playlist in the Source list onto a folder to put it in the folder, and you can take a playlist out of a folder by dragging it to the left edge of the iTunes window.

Adding songs to a playlist:

1. Click Music in the iTunes Source list.

All the content in your Music library is displayed in the main pane of the iTunes window.

2. Click a song to select it.

    You can select multiple songs by Shift-clicking. If your iTunes Library is displaying songs by album cover in iTunes' grid layout, you can select the album by clicking its cover. (To view your Music library in grid layout, choose View > as Grid.)

3. Drag the song to the playlist to which you want to add it.

 You can delete a song from a playlist at any time. First, click the playlist to see its contents; then select the song and press the Delete key. Don't worry—the song is still in your Music library.

Selecting and syncing playlists:

1. Follow steps 1–3 of "Syncing your entire Music library to your iPad" earlier in this project.

2. If they aren't already selected, select the Sync Music check box and the radio button titled Selected playlists, artists, albums, and genres.

3. In the Playlists list, select a folder.

    The Playlists list displays folders before individual playlists, so chances are that your iPad songs folder for this project is near the top, as shown in **Figure 3.26**.

Figure 3.26 Selecting a playlist folder for syncing.

4. Click Apply in the bottom-right corner of the iTunes window.

    iTunes syncs your new playlist, along with any other items selected in the four lists in the music syncing pane (refer to Figure 3.22 earlier in this project).

Get Smart

Aside from playlists and playlist folders, iTunes provides Smart Playlists. When you make a Smart Playlist (by choosing File > Smart Playlist), you specify the conditions that a song must satisfy to be in that playlist. You could specify all songs with the word *Love* in their titles that have been added to your iTunes Music library in the past year, for example. Whatever songs match those conditions end up listed in the playlist. If you add a new song to your Music library that satisfies the Smart Playlist's conditions, it ends up listed in that playlist too.

You can sync Smart Playlists with your iPad, which is why we're bringing the whole topic up. Consult iTunes help for more information about Smart Playlists.

Create a playlist on your iPad

While we're on the subject of playlists, we should point out that you can make a playlist on your iPad, using any of the songs, artists, albums, and genres there. Any playlist that you make on your iPad syncs back to iTunes, where you can modify it and then sync it back to your iPad.

Making a playlist on the iPad:

1. Tap the iPod app's icon on your iPad to open it.

2. Tap Music at the top of the Library column.

   Your Music library appears in a list (**Figure 3.27**).

3. At the bottom of the screen, tap the Songs button; then, in the bottom-left corner, tap the plus (+) icon.

   A New Playlist dialog appears.

4. Enter a name for your playlist, and tap Save.

   Your iPad displays the songs that it contains in alphabetical order and instructs you to add songs to the playlist.

5. Swipe through the list of songs, tapping the ones you want to add to your new playlist.

   As you tap a song's title, it turns gray, indicating that it's been added.

Figure 3.27 All your songs in the iPod on the iPad.

> **tip** You can use the search box at the top of the screen to find the songs you want. You can also use the buttons at the bottom to add albums, artists, genres, and composers.

6. Tap the blue Done button.

Your new playlist appears (**Figure 3.28**).

Figure 3.28 A new iPad playlist awaiting final approval.

7. Tap any song to delete it from the playlist, or tap the playlist in the Library column to delete the whole thing.

8. When the playlist is the way you want it, tap Done again.

Manage your music by hand

Some people like total control of every single item on their iPads, preferring to add and remove songs manually rather than rely on syncing. If you're one of those people, this last section and iTunes' Manually manage music and video option are for you.

The aforementioned setting allows you to drag songs, albums, playlists, videos, and TV shows from your iTunes libraries directly to your iPad's Source list, but it stops iTunes from syncing any of these items automatically. If, for example, you've set iTunes to sync movies you haven't finished watching (see the **Movie and TV-Show Syncing Project** later in this chapter), that syncing capability is disabled when you choose the Manually manage option. *Manually* really does mean *manually*.

Managing music manually:

1. Connect your iPad to your computer.

2. Launch iTunes.

3. Select the iPad in the Source list.

4. Click the Summary button in the main iTunes pane.

5. In the Options section at the bottom of the pane, select Manually manage music and videos.

6. Click Apply in the bottom-right corner of the iTunes window.

Make Your Own E-Books Project

Difficulty level: Intermediate

Software needed: Mac OS X; Scrivener; Microsoft Word, Pages, or another word processor

iPad model: Any

Additional hardware: Mac or Windows PC

Although it's not the only e-book reader for the iPad, iBooks is the "Marian, Madam Librarian" of your iPad's electronic book repository. iBooks recognizes two document formats from the e-book Tower of Babel: ePub and PDF. Adobe introduced PDF to the computer scene in 1993, and in the almost two decades since, PDF documents have become ubiquitous. ePub is newer but based on technology that's every bit as common: XHTML, CSS, and Zip.

The PDF format's downside is that it presents static pages—a concept of fixed dimensions. Therefore, PDFs are less well suited to dynamic presentations, the target audience for which may be using iPads, iPhones, or computer screens (with resizable windows, no less). The upside of the format is that you see the same content in the same type-faces, with the same organization and relative scaling, regardless of the device on which you view it.

ePub is designed for reflowable content, in which readers get the same detail in the same order, fitted to the presentation device.

To summarize, if you receive a PDF "book" of 300 pages on your Mac or Dell PC, it will also be 300 pages on your iPad (or iPhone or iPod touch), and you'll probably need to do the scrolling or deal with the scaling issues yourself. That same 300-page book in ePub format may be 700 pages on your iPad at the default font size and 1,600 pages on your iPhone, but iBooks takes care of the details for you so that you get a seamless rendition irrespective of the viewing platform.

PDF support greatly simplifies the process of putting your own content on the iPad. Using a third-party PDF-creation tool or Mac OS X's built-in printer support for writing PDF files, converting your documents to PDFs is a simple matter of opening them and choosing the right printer or print option. Drag the resulting PDF into iTunes and sync your iPad to make the PDF accessible on the go.

Create a PDF from a document

The following task demonstrates just how simple it is for a Mac user to create a PDF, using the Microsoft Word document for this project as the source.

Creating a PDF:

1. On your computer, open the document in your application of choice.

   For this example, we're using this project file in Microsoft Word 2008.

2. Choose File > Print.

   The Print dialog opens. Ours appears in **Figure 3.29**. Although the basics will be the same, the application and printer you're using could make the dialog sport more or fewer features.

Figure 3.29
The Print dialog.

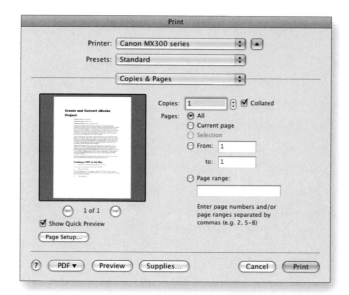

3. Click and hold the PDF button in the bottom-left corner to display the PDF menu (**Figure 3.30**).

Figure 3.30 Use the Print dialog to create PDFs.

4. Choose Save As PDF.

   A Save As dialog appears, letting you name your PDF and specify where it should be saved.

Now you have your PDF, and if you want to, you can drag it into iTunes for syncing to your iPad.

 Microsoft doesn't provide built-in PDF generation in its operating system, but Windows users do have a free solution: CutePDF Writer (www.cutepdf.com/products/cutepdf/writer.asp). You'll need to install the free Ghostscript package; the Web page has links and instructions.

Make an e-book with Scrivener

Creating an ePub document is analogous to creating a PDF, with the primary difference being the final step that renders the content in the desired form. As Shakespeare wrote in *Hamlet,* however, "Therein lies the rub!" Although tools for producing PDF output abound, ePub compilers are less pervasive.

Apple provides one solution: its Pages software (desktop version only), which lets you export your documents in ePub format, which is suitable for use on your iPad, iPhone, or iPod touch.

Although Pages is a very fine word processor and a pretty nifty desktop publishing application too, we prefer Scrivener (www.literatureandlatte. com) when it comes to producing e-books. Scrivener is a writing tool and environment that specifically targets book authors and script-writers. Whereas programs such as Word and Pages focus on creating and formatting documents, Scrivener focuses on creating and organizing content. Until very recently, Scrivener was specific to Mac OS X, but Literature & Latte has released a public beta for Windows.

 The public beta is free but is accompanied by the usual caveats concerning stability. When the tool is released commercially, it will cost $40 ($35 for an educational license). The Mac version is currently priced at $45 but is available for a fully functional free 30-day trial.

Space prohibits us from giving you a Scrivener tutorial here, but the included documentation (a user manual available in the Help menu) is both extensive and coherent, and the video and interactive tutorials should get you up and running in short order.

Creating an e-book with Scrivener:

1. Launch Scrivener.

2. Create a new project.

   For this exercise, you're going to create an ePub of Scrivener's inter-active tutorial, so choose Help > Interactive Tutorial. Follow the prompts, and the Scrivener project opens, fully loaded with the tuto-rial's content.

3. Choose File > Compile.

   The Compile dialog drops down (**Figure 3.31**).

Figure 3.31 Set your output options in the Compile dialog.

4. Choose ePub eBook (.epub) from the Compile For pop-up menu at the bottom of the dialog.

5. Click Contents in the Compilation Options list on the left side of the dialog.

6. In the Pg Break Before column, check the items that you want to include in the table of contents.

To select all items in the list, Option-click the first one.

7. (Optional) In the Meta-Data options, fill in the fields you want the ePub to contain, such as Subject, Description, Publisher, and Publication Date.

8. Click the Compile button.

9. When Scrivener asks you to do so, name the file and specify where you want to save it.

Now that you have your ePub file, you can drag it to iTunes and sync it to your iPad. **Figure 3.32** shows the tutorial saved in iBooks on an iPad, open to the table of contents.

Figure 3.32 Here's the Scrivener interactive tutorial e-book on the iPad.

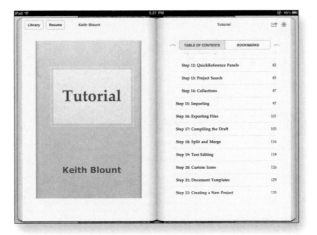

We receive a lot of documentation in HTML, RTF, and Word formats, and we've come to rely on Scrivener to repurpose that documentation into e-books that we can carry around on our iPads and iPhones. Also, reading documentation on our iOS devices is like having lightweight, adjustable second monitors for the documentation while we explore the software on our Macs.

Movie and TV-Show Syncing Project

Difficulty level: Easy

Software needed: iTunes

iPad model: Any

Additional hardware: None

Back in the dawn of time, when we were in film school, movies came in big metal boxes on multiple reels (five or so per movie), and moving a movie from place to place required a very strong back. As for watching that movie, have you ever tried to lug around a 35mm movie projector?

Today, you can carry dozens of movies from place to place in a device that you can lift with your fingertips, and you can watch those movies in glorious high resolution on that same device with a tap of the finger. If you love movies (and we do), today is a Golden Age coated in platinum and sprinkled with diamonds.

In this project, you see how to get movies (and TV shows—we love them too) synced between your iPad and your computer so that no matter where you are, you can get the video fix you crave. No sweat.

Sync movies

Whether you get your movies from the iTunes Store or somewhere else (and we discuss some of the "somewhere else" options elsewhere in this chapter), getting them from your iTunes Library to your iPad and back again isn't rocket science, even though the technology underlying it may be.

You can sync movies in the following ways:

- All movies
- Unwatched movies (*unwatched* movies being those that you haven't watched all the way through to the end)
- The most or least recently obtained unwatched movies
- Selected movies
- Selected playlists of movies

Try Before You Apply

The **Music Syncing Project** earlier in this chapter describes a way for you to manage music and videos manually. If you've set the Manually manage music and videos option in iTunes' Summary pane for your iPad, you can't sync video between your iPad and computer automatically. This project assumes that you *don't* have that option turned on.

When you make any changes in the iTunes syncing panes, the changes don't take effect immediately, so you can try out different settings. When you click something else in the iTunes Source list, iTunes asks whether you want to apply your changes. You can also click Apply in the bottom-right corner of the iTunes window to apply your changes immediately, or you can click Revert to set all your unapplied syncing changes in all the syncing panes back to the way they were (**Figure 3.33**).

Figure 3.33 These two buttons let you apply or ignore syncing changes.

Some of these criteria aren't mutually exclusive. You can sync five recent unwatched movies as well as additional selected movies and playlists of movies, for example.

Also, you can create iTunes playlists that contain movies—especially useful for short movies, such as the ones you make yourself with iMovie or some other movie-creation application.

In this section of the project, you get to experiment with various movie-syncing settings to see how they work.

Turning on movie syncing:

1. Connect your iPad to your computer.

2. Launch iTunes.

3. Select your iPad in the iTunes Source list, below the Devices heading.

4. At the top of the main pane of the iTunes window, click the Movies button.

5. At the top of the Movies pane, select Sync Movies (**Figure 3.34**).

Figure 3.34 This check box is the master key to iPad movie syncing.

When movie syncing is enabled, you have access to the other controls and lists in the Sync Movies section. First, you see how to turn on syncing for all movies.

> **note** If Manually manage music and videos is selected in the Options section of the Summary pane, turning on movie syncing deselects that option. When that happens, the syncing options in the Music pane and TV Shows pane take effect, so you need to look in those panes as well and adjust your syncing options.

Syncing all movies:

1. Below the Sync Movies heading in the Movies pane, click the Automatically include x movies check box.

2. Choose the option titled all from the pop-up menu in the middle of the preceding option's name (**Figure 3.35**).

Figure 3.35 When you sync all movies, the other options in the Movies syncing pane vanish.

The rest of the options in the Movies pane vanish at this point; with all movies set to be synced, you don't need them.

In most cases, you probably *don't* want to sync all your movies, just as you wouldn't pack every piece of clothing you own when you go on a trip. You usually want your iPad to have the newest movies in your collection or the ones that you haven't yet viewed. In the following task, we show you how to make it so.

> **note** Keep in mind that movies take up a lot of room. If you sync all movies, iTunes copies only as many as can fit on your iPad. You may find that you don't have room for many apps, books, or songs if you fill your iPad with movies.

Syncing new or old movies:

1. Below the Sync Movies check box in the Movies pane, check the Automatically include *x* movies option, if it isn't already checked.

2. From the pop-up menu in the middle of the preceding option's name, choose any option other than all or all unwatched (**Figure 3.36**).

Figure 3.36 Your choices for syncing movies automatically.

```
all
1 most recent
3 most recent
5 most recent
10 most recent

all unwatched
1 most recent unwatched
3 most recent unwatched
✓ 5 most recent unwatched
10 most recent unwatched
1 least recent unwatched
3 least recent unwatched
5 least recent unwatched
10 least recent unwatched
```

When you make any choice other than all or all unwatched, all the lists of movies and playlists in the Movies syncing pane become active.

note iTunes uses the date when each movie was added to the iTunes Library—not the movie's release date—to figure out which movies are the most or least recent. From the pop-up menu, you can choose to sync automatically one or more of the most recent watched movies; you can choose one or more of the most recent unwatched movies; or you can choose one or more of the least recent unwatched movies. For some reason, however, you can't choose to sync the least recent watched movies: those, you have to select manually.

Syncing selected movies and movie playlists:

1. Below the Sync Movies check box in the Movies tab, do one of the following things:

   • Clear the Automatically include *x* movies check box.

   • From the pop-up menu in the middle of the Automatically include option's name, choose an item other than all.

   The lists below the option's name become available (**Figure 3.37** on the next page).

Figure 3.37 You can pick movies individually and choose playlists of movies.

2. Click to select the movies you want to include along with your choices from step 1.

 note **If you choose any of the unwatched items from the Automatically include pop-up menu in step 1, you can select only additional movies that don't match the unwatched items you've chosen. The movies that match your choice are automatically selected in the Movies list and can't be deselected.**

3. In the Include Movies from Playlists list (scroll down in the Movies syncing pane to see it), click to select the playlists you want to sync.

Sync TV-show episodes

The videos in your iTunes Library that are categorized as TV shows have two special items of information associated with them that affect syncing: the name of the TV series and the episode of that series. You can use these two pieces of information to specify which TV-show episodes get synced.

The choices you have for syncing TV-show episodes are similar to those for movies:

- All episodes

- Unwatched episodes

- The most or least recently obtained unwatched episodes

- Selected episodes

- Selected playlists that contain TV-show episodes

Because episodes "belong" to TV shows, you can specify whether the unwatched and recent criteria apply to all TV shows or only to selected TV shows. If you're an avid fan of William Daniels, for example, you can choose to sync only the five oldest unwatched episodes of *Captain Nice* and no others.

As with movies, in this part of the project you get to experiment with various syncing settings to see how they work. Also as with movies, any changes you make in TV-show syncing don't take effect without your approval.

Turning on TV-show syncing:

1. Connect your iPad to your computer.

2. Launch iTunes.

3. Select your iPad in the iTunes Source list, below the Devices heading.

4. At the top of the main pane of the iTunes window, click the TV Shows button.

5. At the top of the TV Shows pane, select Sync TV Shows (**Figure 3.38**).

Figure 3.38
Now showing in the TV Shows pane.

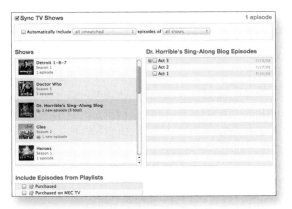

Because TV shows consist of many episodes, only some of which you may have seen, the options for syncing new and old episodes are more flexible than they are for movies, as you see in the following task.

Syncing new or old episodes:

1. Below the Sync TV Shows check box in the TV Shows pane, check the Automatically include *x* episodes of *x* option, if it isn't already checked.

2. From the first pop-up menu in the Automatically include option, choose any item other than all.

3. From the second pop-up menu in the Automatically include option, choose all shows.

   (You deal with selected TV shows a little later in this project.)

4. Select a TV show in the Shows list.

   The Episodes list to the right shows which, if any, of the show's episodes are set to sync automatically (**Figure 3.39**). You can click the check boxes next to other episodes in a show's Episodes list to include those episodes in the sync.

Figure 3.39 You can choose other episodes in addition to those that sync automatically.

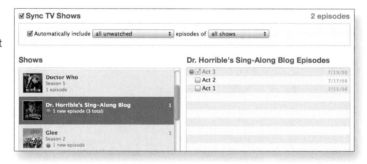

 In addition to the episodes that fall within the syncing criteria you set, you can put TV episodes in playlists and select those playlists in the Include Episodes from Playlists list at the bottom of the TV Shows syncing pane.

Syncing episodes of selected TV shows:

1. Below the Sync TV Shows check box in the TV Shows pane, click the Automatically include option, if it isn't already checked.

2. From the second pop-up menu in the preceding option (the choice in the first pop-up menu doesn't matter), choose selected shows.

   Check boxes appear beside each show's name in the Shows list.

3. In the Shows list, click a show's check box to select it.

   Only the episodes from the selected TV shows that match the criteria in the first pop-up menu sync automatically. As shown in **Figure 3.40**, however, you can select other shows in the Shows list and sync individual episodes of them as well.

Figure 3.40 You can sync episodes from shows other than the ones you've chosen to sync automatically.

Syncing all TV shows:

1. Below the Sync TV Shows check box in the TV Shows pane, click the Automatically include option, if it isn't already checked.

2. From the first pop-up menu in the Automatically include option, choose all.

3. From the second pop-up menu in the Automatically include option, choose all shows.

   All the lists in the TV Shows syncing pane vanish. After all, you don't need these lists if you're syncing everything.

4. In the bottom-right corner of the iTunes window, click Revert.

   In this project, you've been playing around with a lot of settings to see what they do. Unless you want them to take effect—and chances are excellent that you don't—it's best to revert to your original settings and then plan how you *really* want to sync your TV shows and movies. After all, now you know how to do it; that's what this project has been about.

   Happy viewing! But first, stay tuned for these important messages....

What About Music Videos?

In addition to TV shows and movies, you may have music videos in your iTunes Library—videos that were included with albums you purchased or that you purchased individually. Music videos sync according to the same criteria you set for the songs in your Music library—*if* you set the right music syncing option.

In the Music syncing pane, in the first group of options, select the Include music videos option. That's it. Now when you sync your music, your music videos come along for the ride. You'll find them on your iPad in the Video app's Music Videos category.

Moving Movie Rentals

You can't sync movies that you've rented from the iTunes Store on your computer. You can *move* rentals from your computer to your iPad and back, but the rental is always on only one device at a time.

In addition, if you rent a movie from the iTunes Store on your iPad, it stays on your iPad; you can't move it to your computer or any other device. (Similarly, if you rent a movie via AppleTV, you can't move it from AppleTV to any other device.)

Streaming Internet Video Project

Difficulty level: Intermediate

Software needed: ABC Player (free), Netflix app (free)

iPad model: Any

Additional hardware: None

Everywhere we turn, we find people catching TV shows at times other than the scheduled broadcast times and, frequently, on devices other than a TV set. Battling viewership loss to cable, and in an attempt to recoup ad revenue lost to cable and other competition, network television has begun to embrace alternative delivery systems—in particular, the Internet and iTunes.

Time and venue shifting have become so pervasive that Nielsen Media Research, in an attempt to stay relevant, purchased NetRatings to measure the demographics of the rapidly growing Internet viewing population. Nielsen also factors iTunes and YouTube viewing into its ratings.

Also, Netflix, the Big Kahuna of video rental, is deemphasizing sending DVD and Blu-ray discs by mail in favor of streaming rentals to customers' Web browsers or mobile devices. As we all know, the best mobile device for receiving these rentals is the iPad. For $7.99 per month, you can watch an awful lot of video without making a single trip to rental sites or the mailbox.

Get the TV software

Although all the networks stream their shows via their Web sites, and though Safari on the iPad provides a competent content conduit, ABC has taken things a step further, providing a dedicated iPad app called ABC Player to stream its shows to handheld devices.

This app offers a viewing experience that's tailored to the iPad rather than the lowest-common-denominator Web browser interface—as you see in **Figure 3.41** and **Figure 3.42**, which were taken seconds apart on the same day.

Figure 3.41 ABC's Web interface.

Figure 3.42 ABC Player's interface.

Obtaining ABC Player:

1. Tap the App Store icon on your iPad's home screen.

2. In the Search field in the top-right corner of the App Store's home screen, type **ABC**; then tap ABC Player in the list that appears.

3. Tap the ABC Player entry (which should appear in the top-left corner of the iPad Apps section).

   The ABC Player product page appears.

4. Tap the Free button below the icon in the top-left corner.

   Free flips over and becomes Install.

5. Tap Install.

6. When you're asked to enter your Apple ID and password, do so.

   You're back at the home screen, and ABC Player is downloading. You're ready to start enjoying ABC's network TV shows. (At least, ABC hopes that you'll enjoy them.) Tap the ABC Player icon to enter the world of ABC prime-time (and more) television.

Use ABC Player

When you have ABC Player running, you find five buttons along the bottom of the screen: Featured, Schedule, All Shows, Me, and Info (refer to **Figure 3.42** earlier in this project).

Viewing ABC's featured favorites:

1. If it isn't already selected (as it is by default), tap the Featured button at the bottom of the ABC Player screen.

   You see a large thumbnail at the top of the screen, displaying a show that ABC is—wait for it—featuring (**Figure 3.43**). This display slides to the left about every 5 seconds to bring a new show's thumbnail into view.

2. To speed the movement of the large thumbnail display or to make it go in the opposite direction, touch the thumbnail and then flick your finger in the desired direction.

Figure 3.43
ABC's featured shows and episodes on a spring day in 2011. Your mileage may vary.

3. To watch a recent episode, do one of the following things:

   • To watch the most recent episode of a series during its regular season, tap the Watch Latest Episode button to—yes—watch the latest episode of that show.

   • To watch the first episode of a new series (like *Body of Proof* in Figure 3.43), tap the Watch the Series Premiere! button.

   • To watch episodes of a series that's between seasons, tap the button labeled Catch Up on Season *n* (where *n* is the number of the just-completed season).

4. To view a specific episode of one of the shows displayed below the scrolling thumbnail, tap that episode's thumbnail.

5. To modify what's being displayed in the various thumbnails, tap Most Popular, Most Recent, or Staff Picks.

Figure 3.44 Pick an ABC episode from the weekly calendar display.

Seeing what's on the schedule:

1. To check out the network schedule, tap the Schedule button at the bottom of the ABC Player screen.

    You see a screen resembling the one shown in **Figure 3.44**.

2. Tap the desired day of the week to find that day's shows in their ABC time slots.

    As you can see in Figure 3.44, some shows aren't available for viewing on the iPad—usually, local broadcasts, sporting events, and the like. Also, shows that are available in the iTunes Store are so marked, with a button you can tap to buy them.

Checking it all:

1. Tap the All Shows button at the bottom of the ABC Player screen.

    You see a grid of all available ABC shows (**Figure 3.45**).

2. Tap a show's thumbnail to see a pop-up list of episodes (**Figure 3.46**).

3. Tap the desired episode to start viewing.

Figure 3.45 Find the show you want in ABC's All Shows grid.

Figure 3.46 Tap the show to see a list of available episodes.

Reviewing your viewing history:

1. Tap the Me button at the bottom of the ABC Player screen.

   You see a thumbnail (or grid of thumbnails) representing the episode(s) you've seen so far At the top of each thumbnail is a timeline, with a down-pointing arrow showing where you left off watching the episode (**Figure 3.47**). Near the top-right corner of each thumbnail is a small x that you can tap to remove the episode from your history.

Figure 3.47 Check here in case you don't remember what you've already watched (or if you like reruns).

2. (Optional) If you see an episode you want to watch again or want to pick up watching an episode where you left off, tap its thumbnail.

 This feature is great if you regularly watch a few TV series and have seen multiple episodes of each one. It's very easy to lose track of which episodes you've viewed and which you haven't. Thanks to the Me button, you don't have to remember multiple episode names in multiple series.

Giving ABC feedback:

1. Tap the Info button at the bottom of the ABC Player screen.

   A feedback form appears (**Figure 3.48**). This form is a lot less colorful than the player's other pages, but you hold sway here.

Figure 3.48 Tell ABC what you think, or make suggestions.

2. Fill out the form to tell ABC what you consider to be good or bad, or to suggest features you'd like to see in future versions.

3. When you've had your say, tap the Send Feedback button.

View the video stream

After you tap an episode in the Featured, Schedule, All Shows, or Me screen (well, some people like to watch shows multiple times, so if you're not one of them, you don't need to tap an episode in your history), ABC Player starts loading the episode.

During the loading process, the player displays a placard stating that the following episode is being presented with limited commercials. That may be true, especially if you're defining *limited* by counting the distinct advertising spots, because you generally get the same two or three commercials repeated ad nauseam through the show. It also may be true if your tolerance for interruptions is greater than ours. We count four interruptions per hourlong episode in addition to the lead-in commercials, with two commercials per interruption. (Actually, an "hourlong" episode viewed in ABC Player is typically 42 to 43 minutes long, not counting commercials, but that's the norm for network television these days.)

When the introductory commercial break is over, the episode starts to play.

Controlling video playback:

1. While you're viewing an episode in ABC Player, tap a video to display viewing controls at the bottom of the screen (**Figure 3.49**).

Playhead

Figure 3.49 Tap an episode to control its playback.

Play/Pause button   Timeline   Letterbox/Full Screen button

Done button

2. Do any of the following things:

   - Tap the blue Done button to go back to the show's episode screen.

   - Tap the Play/Pause button to toggle between playing and pausing.

   - Tap the Letterbox/Full Screen button to control the video's aspect ratio.

   - Drag the playhead in the timeline to move to a different point in the episode.

note   **Be aware, however, that if you drag over one of the tick marks (each of which denotes a "limited commercial interruption"), the playhead lands on the commercial rather than on the particular point you chose.**

Commercials More Annoying Than on Disc or on Demand

When a commercial is playing, the viewing controls are inaccessible. You can't pause playback, much less fast-forward or rewind. In fact, you can't even end playback and return to the selection page.

This situation is particularly annoying when you accidentally tap one of the thumbnails, because every video starts with one of these uninterruptible commercials. Thus, you have to sit through the commercial until the controls are available again—or press the iPad's Home button, then double-press the Home button to display the process bar, hold one of the app icons until all the icons wiggle, tap the X in ABC Player's top-left corner to terminate the process, and then relaunch the ABC Player app. (Owners of this book's first edition may note that the advent of multitasking made this procedure a bit longer.)

Watch movies and TV on demand

Netflix introduced flat-rate DVD rental by mail, letting subscribers create lists of what they wanted to see and get those DVDs in their mailboxes (with prepaid return envelopes) so that steady streams of discs were wending their way back and forth.

A few years ago, the company tested the waters of streaming video, letting subscribers watch their videos over the Internet for a flat monthly fee. As more and more people have acquired broadband connections to the Internet, the viable customer base for online service has increased, to the point that most of Netflix's business now is online. An online subscription costs $7.99 per month and lets you have unlimited rentals on your iPad, iPhone, iPod touch, and/or computer.

 Be aware, though, that what's available for online viewing is only a subset of what's available on DVD. Further, at the time we're writing this chapter, HD content isn't available via online subscription. Finally, the Netflix app doesn't yet support AirPlay, so if you want to view what's streaming on a larger screen, you need a composite, component, or digital connector kit (as appropriate for your TV set).

Make sure that you have a good wireless signal and a fast Internet connection when you're viewing streaming video, as a weak signal or erratic connection can easily result in poor picture and sound quality.

Getting started with Netflix:

1. Purchase the Netflix app from the App Store, if you haven't already.

2. Tap the Netflix app's icon to launch it on your iPad.

    The login page opens (**Figure 3.50**).

Figure 3.50 Log in to your Netflix account, or create one.

3. Do one of the following:

    •   If you already have a Netflix account, enter your email address and password, and tap the Sign In button.

    •   If you don't have an account, tap the Netflix.com link. Safari ferries you to the Netflix site, where you can sign up.

Picking a genre and movie to watch:

1. Log in to Netflix, and select the Genres tab (**Figure 3.51** on the next page), and tap the genre that interests you.

    A selection of titles in the selected genre appears.

Figure 3.51 Specify the kind of movie you want to view.

 tip   **If you select the Home tab instead, you see a New Releases screen, listing new movies and TV shows.**

2. Tap a movie's title.

   The movie's Info screen appears, presenting a brief description and buttons you can tap to add the movie to your queue or play it.

3. Do one of the following:

   - **Tap the Play button.** Netflix spins the wait cursor for a few seconds and then starts playing your selection.

   - **Tap the Add to Instant button.** Netflix adds the movie to a list of movies you want to watch when you get a chance.

Searching for video:

1. Log in to Netflix, and select the Search tab.

2. Type key words in the Search box.

   Netflix presents a list of matches (**Figure 3.52**). Some matches are marked as being unavailable, however, and others are marked as being available only via disc subscription (for an additional $2 per month and a lack of instant gratification).

Figure 3.52
Sometimes Netflix tells you about titles that you can't stream, along with the ones you can.

3. Tap the title of something that is available.

   That movie's Info screen appears.

4. Do one of the following:

   - **Tap the Play button.** Netflix spins the wait cursor for a few seconds and then starts playing your selection.

   - **Tap the Add to Instant button.** Netflix adds the movie to a list of movies you want to watch when you get a chance.

Playing what's queued:

1. Log in to Netflix, and select the Instant Queue tab.

   Netflix displays the items in your queue (**Figure 3.53**).

Figure 3.53
This screen displays the movies and TV shows you've put in your waiting list.

2. Tap the title you want to view.

    If you select a movie, it starts playing. If you select a TV series, you see a list of episodes; tap the Play button for the one you want to view (**Figure 3.54**).

Figure 3.54 Select an episode of a queued TV series.

3G Users, Beware!

Unless you're rich as Crœsus or consider AT&T or Verizon to be your favorite charity, you should be very careful about streaming video (other than an occasional short clip) over a 3G connection. Video comprises a lot of data, especially HD video, and you can rapidly exceed your monthly data allotment in a 3G contract, whether that amount is 250 MB, 1 GB, or 2 GB. A single 2-hour movie could easily consume your monthly allotment and have you paying a hefty overage penalty to boot.

If you're going to watch streaming video (and we think that streaming video falls into the "good things in life" category), make sure that you're viewing it over a Wi-Fi connection.

Make a Movie Project

Difficulty level: Easy

Software needed: iMovie app ($4.99)

iPad model: iPad 2

Additional hardware: None

Apple led the way in personal-computer video creation when it released the iMac DV and iMovie in 1999. iMovie has gone through multiple iterations but has consistently been reviewed as a compelling combination of power and ease of use. The latest version of iMovie—for the iPad 2, iPhone 4, and iPod touch (fourth generation)—is adapted to the iOS touchscreen interface for the low, low price of just $4.99.

This version has some drawbacks. You can't edit any video other than what you've taken with an iOS device, for example—nothing that you've downloaded from the Internet, received in email, or acquired from anything other than another iOS device. One nice touch, though, is that you don't have to have a wired connection to your Mac or PC running iTunes to transfer an iMovie project. If you have a wireless connection, you can use iTunes File Sharing to save a project to iTunes from an iPhone or iPod touch; retrieve that content on your iPad; and edit the project there to take advantage of the iPad's larger screen.

In this project, you use Apple's iMovie app to assemble your video clips and photos into a movie, with optional background music and narration, and then share it with friends and family, post it to the Internet, or just keep it for your own reference or enjoyment.

Get your project started

All right, you have some video segments you've shot with your iPad's cameras, and you want to turn them into a movie. The following task shows you how.

 To access iMovie's integrated help system, tap the question-mark icon in the bottom-left corner of an iMovie screen. Just about anything you may want to know about the various controls and features are well covered in this help system, but it doesn't provide a "Getting Started" tutorial, so that's what we're providing in this first section.

Starting the movie:

1. If you don't have the iMovie app installed on your iPad, go to the App Store and purchase it ($4.99 at this writing).

2. Tap the iMovie icon on your iPad's home screen.

    You see the My Projects screen, shown in **Figure 3.55**. This screen is your project gallery.

Figure 3.55 iMovie's My Projects screen, waiting for you to create your first project.

3. Tap the plus sign in the center of the screen, as directed, to create a new project.

    A new My Project screen opens (**Figure 3.56**). The top-left pane shows content that's available to be added to your project—in Figure 3.56, a short video clip, shot with the iPad's camera, that resides in the Camera Roll album.

Figure 3.56 A new project, waiting for you to start creating and editing your movie.

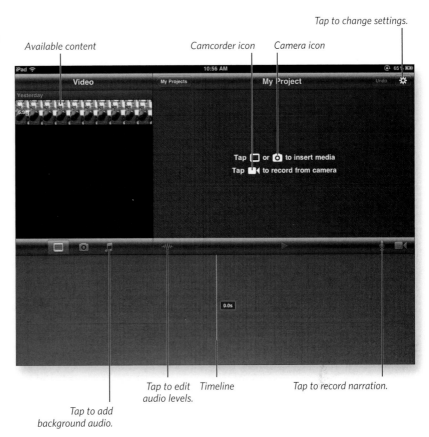

Available content

Camcorder icon

Camera icon

Tap to change settings.

Tap to add background audio.

Tap to edit audio levels.

Timeline

Tap to record narration.

4. To add some footage to your project, do one (or more) of the following:

- **Tap a video clip to select it.** An orange outline appears around the selected clip, and a curved arrow appears in the center of the clip. Tap the arrow, and iMovie moves the clip into the timeline at the bottom of the screen.

- **Tap the camera icon to select a still image.** Navigate through your photos to find a still image that you want to add to the timeline (a handy way to create a slideshow). **Figure 3.57** (on the next page) shows the project with both a video clip and a still image in the timeline.

- **Tap the camcorder icon to record video for direct insertion into the timeline.** You're using the Camera app from within iMovie, with access to all the expected features (front or back camera, still or video recording). Tap the Done button when you finish shooting or filming, and you return to the My Project screen, with your freshly shot footage added to the timeline.

5. (Optional) Tap the musical-notes icon above the timeline (refer to Figure 3.56) to add background audio to your project.

6. (Optional) Tap the gear icon (refer to Figure 3.56) to change various settings, such as the theme.

    The Project Settings popover opens (**Figure 3.58**).

Figure 3.57 You can turn still images into short video segments.

Figure 3.58 Pick a theme and establish your project settings here.

 note In the Project Settings popover shown in Figure 3.58, background audio has been added to the timeline; the green background represents the duration of the audio.

7. (Optional) Tap the waveform icon (refer to Figure 3.56) to edit audio levels.

8. (Optional) Tap the microphone icon (refer to Figure 3.56) to record narration.

    An overlay displaying your audio level (volume) and a Record button appears (**Figure 3.59**).

Tap Record, and after a 3-second countdown, recording begins. Tap the Stop button when you finish; then tap Discard, Retake, Review, or Accept in the resulting display (**Figure 3.60**).

Figure 3.59 Ready to start recording narration.

Figure 3.60 Decide what to do with your most recent narrative take.

9. When you have the project the way you want it, return to the original My Projects screen by tapping the My Projects button at the top-center of the My Project screen.

   Your project is front and center in the My Projects screen below a "Now Playing" marquee that lists the project's name.

Give your project a name

Although *My Project* could be a functional movie title, it isn't as compelling as *The High and the Mighty* or even as descriptive as *Marcus's Little League Opener*. You really want to add an evocative title so that you can find the movie easily later.

Naming your movie:

1. Tap the project title in the marquee to select it.

   The project's title is highlighted, and the virtual keyboard appears (**Figure 3.61** on the next page).

Figure 3.61
Selected project.

2. Tap the little *x* at the right end of the highlighted area.

   The current title disappears.

3. Type your new project title.

Fill your distribution channels

Sometimes, people create videos for their own use, but most movies are created for a wider audience: friends, family members, or the world at large. Now that the project has a name, it's time to determine where you want it to be distributed. iMovie makes it easy for you to send the project to several video-sharing sites.

Sharing your movie:

1. Tap the curved-arrow Action button at the bottom of the My Project screen.

   A popover appears, listing six common destinations (**Figure 3.62**).

Figure 3.62 Pick a place to send your video.

2. Tap one of the destinations:

   - **Camera Roll** saves your movie in your iPad's Camera Roll album in your choice of three sizes (**Figure 3.63**). Then you can view it in the Photos app, share it via email or MobileMe, or sync it back to your Mac or PC.

Figure 3.63 Choose a size for the video you're saving to the Camera Roll album.

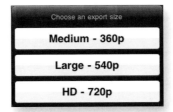

   - **YouTube** is the 800-pound gorilla of modern video sharing. You need a free account to post your movies on YouTube.

   - **Facebook** is the preeminent social-networking site of the day. If you have a free Facebook membership, you can host your movies on your personal page for your friends and acquaintances to view and comment on.

   - **Vimeo** is another popular video-sharing site, best known for leading the way in hosting high-definition video, White House broadcasts, and famous performers' work. The basic (and limited) membership is free; the Plus membership currently costs $60 per year.

- **CNN iReport** lets everyday folk submit videos about breaking news. It's a sort of news wiki, without any fact-checking or peer review.

- **iTunes** lets you save your project via iTunes File Sharing so that it's accessible to other iPads, iPhones, and iPod touches.

 If you want your movie to go to multiple destinations, you need to choose them one at a time, because each destination requires its own settings or sign-in process.

Streaming Your Own Video Project

Difficulty level: Intermediate

Software needed: Air Video ($2.99) or Air Video Free (free), Air Video Server (free)

iPad model: Any

Additional hardware: Mac or Windows computer

We love TV and movies, and the iPad is a fantastic platform on which to watch our video. Unfortunately, the iPad's Videos and iPod apps don't support most of the formats in which video is commonly distributed. The iPad likes only MPEG-4 (MP4 or M4V). It doesn't like several common formats that you'd need to transcode to play on your iPad, including MPEG-1 and MPEG-2 (used for VCDs [video compact discs] and DVDs); QuickTime; AVI, DivX, and Xvid (the last two are also MPEG-4, but not the preferred variant); Matroska (MKV); and Adobe Flash. Transcoding every one of these formats involves a diminution of quality resulting from recompression to the new format.

Add to that fact this consideration: Video takes a lot of space, and your iPad's storage space is fairly limited. Your desktop (or laptop) computer, on the other hand, usually has a pretty large hard drive, and you can extend that space with additional drives. Wouldn't it be nice to use your iPad to view the video stored on your computer without having to sync it? Thanks to InMethod's Air Video products, you can do just that. Read on.

Get Air Video

You need two pieces of InMethod software:

- **Air Video or Air Video Free.** You can get Air Video at www.inmethod.com or from the App Store. If Air Video's $2.99 price tag puts you off, or if you just feel compelled to try before you buy, you can obtain Air Video Free (available from the same sources), which limits the number of videos accessible in each folder.

- **Air Video Server.** You also need the free server software, available at www.inmethod.com. Air Video Server requires Mac OS X 10.5 (Leopard) or later, or Windows XP Service Pack 3 or later (the same Windows software required for iPad support).

Air Video streams virtually any video on your computer's hard drive, transcoding it as necessary. The lone exception is copy-protected video, which you usually purchase or rent from the iTunes Store (see the nearby "Copy Protection and DRM" sidebar, if you're curious).

 Although Air Video transcodes on the fly, which is the way that most users employ it, you can perform the conversions before streaming the content. If you have a slower network (or a computer slower than a Core 2 Duo), you may want to perform the up-front conversion.

Copy Protection and DRM

Rather than call it *copy-protected*—a term that has serious negative connotations in the public mind—the music and movie industries refer to this type of content as *digital rights management* (DRM) content.

Copy protection and DRM are the same thing when you're dealing with digital material. Because the DRM content you obtain from the iTunes Store is already in an iPad-compatible format, and you can sync it to your iPad, why can't Air Video stream it? Well, the DRM license that the lawyers impose on Apple precludes streaming of DRM content except in controlled (and negotiated) situations, such as AppleTV and AirPlay through iTunes. Therefore, if you want to watch video from the iTunes Store on your iPad using Air Video, that's about the only video that Air Video *won't* handle and that you'll have to sync to view. (AirPlay will stream the video from iTunes on your local network, but the content isn't available over the Internet, as in the case of Air Video.)

Obtaining the Air Video software:

1. Point your Web browser to www.inmethod.com.

2. Click the button labeled Get Air Video from the iTunes App Store, or click the link for the free version.

3. In the App Store, follow the familiar steps to complete your acquisition and download the app to your iTunes Library.

4. Sync your iPad so that the software is installed on your iPad.

 You can combine steps 2–4 by connecting to the App Store on your iPad and making the purchase there. Remember that Air Video won't be backed up to your computer until your next sync.

5. Back on the InMethod Web site, click the graphic for your operating system (the blue Apple logo if you're using a Mac or the Windows logo if that's your platform) to download the Air Video Server software for your computer.

    The Server software for your platform downloads and installs itself on your computer.

 If the Server software doesn't install automatically when you download it, run the installer (Windows) or drag the Server application's icon to your Applications folder (Mac).

Introduce your iPad to Air Video Server

Now that you have Air Video on your iPad and Air Video Server on your computer, it's time to open the lines of communication.

Setting up Air Video Server:

1. Launch Air Video Server.

    You should see the dialog shown in **Figure 3.64**.

Figure 3.64 The Air Video Server Preferences dialog.

2. If you want to specify a folder (such as your Movies folder on a Mac or your MyMovies folder in Windows), click the Add Folder button, and navigate in the Open dialog to select your folder.

   Now your specified folder appears in the dialog's list box, as shown in **Figure 3.65**.

Figure 3.65 Your first entry in the folders that Air Video can access.

3. Repeat step 2 for any additional folders you want to make available.

   Note that selecting a folder makes all subordinate folders accessible.

4. To add iTunes playlists to the list of streamable locations, click the Add iTunes Playlist button.

   The iTunes Playlists dialog opens (**Figure 3.66**).

Figure 3.66 Select any iTunes playlists you want to access.

note As we mention earlier in this project, copy-protected content from the iTunes Store won't stream. iTunes playlists are handy for your home videos, iTunes U courseware, video podcasts, and other content that lacks DRM.

5. Select the iTunes playlists (or categories) you want to add, and click Add.

   You return to the Air Video Server Preferences dialog.

6. Make sure that the Server Running switch at the top of the window is set to Yes, as shown in **Figure 3.67**.

   Air Video Server runs as a background process. No icon for it appears in either the Mac OS X Dock or the Windows taskbar. If you close the window, the application continues to run, and a dialog (**Figure 3.68**) informs you that you can still access it via an icon in the main menu bar (Mac) or system tray (Windows).

   You're good to go and should find your specified content available in the Air Server app on your iPad (**Figure 3.69**).

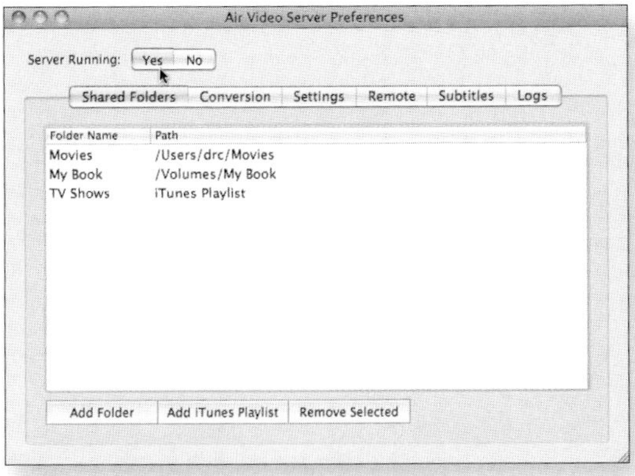

Figure 3.67 Make sure that Server is turned on.

Figure 3.68 Use the menu-bar or system-tray icon to access the faceless Server application.

Figure 3.69 Your selected folders and their contents are now available on your iPad.

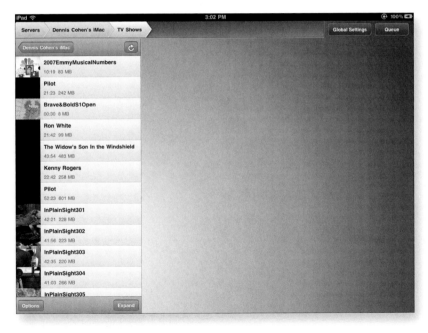

Setting Additional Server Preferences

In the Air Video Server Preferences dialog (refer to Figure 3.64 earlier in this project), you can click the other tabs to set various preferences that launch the application automatically at login, require a password, or set a custom port (Settings tab).

You can also instruct Server to honor Internet access (Remote tab), but this functionality requires that your router support UPnP (Universal Plug and Play) or NAT-PMP (Network Address Translation-Port Mapping Protocol). When you select the Enable Access from Internet check box, a server PIN is displayed. Make certain that the Automatically Map Port check box is selected. Now you can access Air Video Server from remote locations via Wi-Fi or (if Wi-Fi isn't available and you have a 3G iPad) via AT&T's or Verizon's 3G network.

Caution: 3G access is slower than Wi-Fi, so live conversion may be more problematic. Also, with AT&T's and Verizon's pricing, the amount of data video involved can burn through your monthly 3G allotment fast, causing you to run up some hefty overage charges.

Play your content

Playing your content is simple, just as you'd expect on the iPad. Air Video's iPad user interface operates in landscape orientation, even when the iPad is vertical. We find this fact somewhat amusing because Air Video started as an iPhone app and the iPhone user interface is portrait, even though playback is landscape.

At any rate, if you're using your iPad in portrait orientation, rotate it 90 degrees to landscape or tilt your head 90 degrees (if you don't mind being uncomfortable).

Playing a video:

1. Select the video you want to play, tunneling down through your folder hierarchy if necessary.

   The beginning of your video appears in the preview pane on the right side of the iPad screen (**Figure 3.70**).

   You can tap the Play with Live Conversion button if you're into immediate gratification; tap the Convert button if you're a disciple of

Job; or, if the content is available in a compatible form, tap the Play button to stream it without having to do any conversion.

Figure 3.70 The preview pane includes controls that start your video, convert your video, and manage the conversion queue.

2. For the purposes of this task, choose to be impatient, and tap Play with Live Conversion.

   After a quick spin of the wait cursor, your video starts to play in the preview pane.

tip **If you do elect to perform a conversion before you play the video, you can check the queued conversions and their status by tapping the Queue button in the top-right corner of the preview pane.**

3. Tap the double-arrow button in the bottom-right corner of the preview pane (**Figure 3.71**) to have your video appear full screen, if it doesn't transition to full screen automatically.

Figure 3.71 When video is playing, controls are available at the bottom of the preview pane.

— *Full Screen button*

4. In the controller overlay (**Figure 3.72**), do any of the following:

Elapsed time   Scrubber   Timeline   *Remaining time*

Figure 3.72 Video displayed in full-screen mode and the controls available in that mode.

30-Second Rewind   *Advance* | *Full Screen*

Play/Pause   *Volume*

- Tap the 30-Second Rewind button to go backward in 30-second increments.

- Tap the Play/Pause button to switch from playing to pausing, and vice versa.

- Tap the Advance button to move to the next chapter marker (or the end of the video, if the video has no remaining chapter markers).

- Tap the Full Screen button again if you want to go back to the screen with the preview pane (refer to Figure 3.71).

- Drag the scrubber in the timeline to move to any point in the video you want. The current time code (how far into the video you are) is shown at the left end of the timeline, and the remaining time in the video is displayed at the right end.

With the release of iOS 4.3 (coincident with the iPad 2's debut), Air Video will play your videos over AirPlay in the background, so you can stream your content to an AppleTV-equipped HD television set.

More Convenience Features

Here are a few tips for added enjoyment and functionality:

- If the controls aren't visible, just tap within the video to make them appear.

- Double-tap the video in full-screen mode, and the video expands to fill the screen, even if that expansion results in cropping the sides of a widescreen show. You can do the same thing by tapping the Full Screen button (refer to Figure 3.71), switching between letterbox and full-screen view.

- If you've added videos to or removed videos from the folder currently displayed in the list on the left side of the preview pane, tap the Refresh button in the top-right corner of the list (refer to Figure 3.70) to update the display.

Home Sharing Project

Difficulty level: Easy to intermediate

Software needed: iTunes (free), AirView (free)

iPad model: Any

Additional hardware: Another iOS 4.3 device (iPhone, iPod touch, iPad), AppleTV, Mac or PC

Long before the iPhone or iPad came to be, Apple introduced AirTunes, which supported streaming the music from a Mac or Windows PC running iTunes to remote speakers on a wireless network. (This feature sold a fair number of AirPort Express wireless units.) Later came AppleTV, which supported streaming video and audio content from computers to high-definition TV sets, as well as direct access to the iTunes Store for content. In iTunes 10, Apple upped the ante. The resulting feature, Home Sharing, let users share iTunes content with other wireless devices in a home network.

In iOS 4.3, Apple introduced AirPlay, which once again raises the bar. Now, in addition to sharing what's in a computer's iTunes Library, you can stream the content from one AirPlay-capable device to another—from your iPad to another iPad, an iPhone, or AppleTV, for example.

Although Home Sharing and AirPlay may seem to be similar, they're quite different technologies:

- Home Sharing emanates strictly from a computer running iTunes. Other wireless devices on the home network request content from the computer. (Dennis's iMac, for example, frequently streams video to AppleTV while his wife accesses songs from the garden.)

- AirPlay, on the other hand is a broadcast model. You start something playing on your computer or iPad, iPhone, or iPod touch, and AirPlay-capable devices pluck the stream from the air.

At this writing, you can't receive an AirPlay broadcast on a computer.

Stream from one iOS device to another

AirPlay, with the assistance of the free AirView app, lets you stream audio and video from a computer running iTunes or an iOS device to an iOS device running AirView or to any AirPlay-compliant receiver, such as AppleTV or remote speakers (with AirPlay circuitry or an AirPort Express connection). You might think of AirPlay as being a way to redirect the audio or video you're playing.

AirPlay-capable speakers are available from manufacturers such as Denon, Marantz, and iHome. Bloomberg reports that AirPlay-capable devices such as TVs are coming in 2011, but no announcements were made while we were writing this book.

In the following section, we demonstrate streaming video from one iPad to another. (You can also stream from an iPad to an iPhone, an iPod touch, or AppleTV, but because you're reading *The iPad 2 Project Book,* the following task is all iPad.)

Streaming from iPad to iPad:

1.   If you don't have AirView installed, go to the App Store and down-
     load it.

2.   On the iPad that will receive the stream, tap the AirView app's icon
     to get it running.

     You should see the screen shown in **Figure 3.73**.

Figure 3.73 AirView is
waiting to be served
some content.

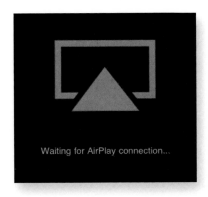

Waiting for AirPlay connection...

3.   On the iPad that contains the content you want to stream, start
     playing that content.

4.   In the control strip at the bottom of the screen, tap the AirPlay
     button (**Figure 3.74**).

Figure 3.74
The AirPlay button lets
you select a destina-
tion device.

AirPlay button

     A pop-up menu appears, listing all the devices that are AirPlay clients.

5.   Tap the destination iPad.

     Your video (or audio) stops playing on the originating iPad and starts
     playing on the destination iPad.

**You can't use AirPlay to transmit digital rights management (DRM)
material, as we discuss in the *Streaming Your Own Video Project* earlier
in this chapter.**

You can use Air Video and AirPlay to stream convert-on-the-fly content to AppleTV with the help of Air Video Server 2.4.5 or later. At this writing, this method is the only known way to view certain types of content (Adobe Flash, DivX, MKV, and so on) via AppleTV.

Share your iTunes Library

Almost from the start, iTunes has supported sharing an iTunes Library from one Mac or PC to other computers. The addition of Home Sharing takes this functionality one step further. Now you can access your iTunes content not only on other computers, but also on any iOS device that contains your iTunes Store account information.

After an iTunes Library is set up as a server, all activity is initiated by devices on the network. Therefore, you can't use Home Sharing to get content to AppleTV or to wireless speakers, which have no user interface for requesting data.

Accessing a shared iTunes Library on an iPad:

1. Launch iTunes on your Mac or PC.

2. Turn on Home Sharing by choosing Advanced > Turn On Home Sharing.

3. Enter your Apple ID and password in the Home Sharing screen (**Figure 3.75**), and click the Create Home Share button.

Figure 3.75 The Home Sharing screen.

![Home Sharing screen showing the Home Sharing logo, explanatory text, Apple ID and Password fields, and No, Thanks and Create Home Share buttons.]

🏠 **Home Sharing**

Home Sharing helps you manage your family's iTunes collection, by copying iTunes Store purchases among computers in your home. iTunes can automatically copy new purchases, or you can choose the items you want to copy.

An Apple ID is required to use Home Sharing. Use the same account for all shared computers.

Apple ID: [redacted]
Password: •••••••
Need an Apple ID? ⊕

No, Thanks   Create Home Share

4. Do one of the following things:

- Open your iPad's iPod app, tap the Library entry to open a Home Sharing popover, and choose the library from which you intend to share audio (**Figure 3.76**).

Figure 3.76
Choose the library from which you want to retrieve songs.

- Open your iPad's Video app, tap the Shared tab, and choose the library from which you intend to play video (**Figure 3.77**). (We had only one shared library at the time we wrote this project, so that's what you see in the figure.)

Figure 3.77 Select the library from which you want to retrieve video in the Shared pane.

5. At the top of the resulting screen, tap the tab that represents the type of content you want to share: Movies, TV Shows, Podcasts, Music Videos, or iTunes U (**Figure 3.78**).

Figure 3.78 Select the category of the content you want to play.

6. Tap the thumbnail that represents the actual content you want to share; then tap the Play button that appears.

   The content starts to play on your iPad.

When you close iTunes on a computer that's serving Home Sharing content, all connections are severed. Therefore, if you want to continue sharing the iTunes Library, don't quit iTunes, log out, or shut down the serving computer.

Index